The Tragedie of Anthonie and Cleopatra

By Edward de Vere

Art:
Portrait of Edward de Vere
17th Earl of Oxford (1550-1604)

This edition produced by
Verus Publishing

www.verusbooks.com

Copyright 2019 Verus Publishing
This book, with the exception of the text of the play itself, remains the copyrighted property of the publisher and may not be duplicated or redistributed in whole or in part without express permission.

ISBN: 978-1-951267-27-8
Imprint / Publisher: Verus Publishing

The Author

Edward de Vere, 17th Earl of Oxford

Biography and Bibliography
After the Play

A Preverse

Drone on ye learned scholars of the day
As to with whom the words ahead the credit lay.
For our part though can be no further doubt
That the author of these words has been found out
To be a person lordly and refined
On whom the light of wit so boldly shined
That to keep this wit from tearing in the fray
He gave another, lesser wit his say.

Now let the least of wits
That writes these paltry lines
Yield to him whose peerless name
Should be with reverence spake.
Let this name be not of history's misassigns
Whose pen and verse have made the earth to shake.

The Tragedie of Anthonie and Cleopatra

By Edward de Vere

The Main Characters

Mark Antony – Roman general and one of the three joint leaders, or "triumvirs", who rule the Roman Republic after the assassination of Julius Caesar in 44 B.C.

Octavius Caesar – another triumvir

Lepidus – another triumvir

Cleopatra – Queen of Egypt

Sextus Pompey – rebel against the triumvirate and son of the late Pompey

Antony's party

Demetrius
Philo
Domitius Enobarbus
Ventidius
Silius – officer in Ventidius' army

Eros
Canidius – Antony's lieutenant-general
Scarus
Dercetus
Schoolmaster – Antony's ambassador to Octavius
    Rannius (non-speaking role)
    Lucilius (non-speaking role)
    Lamprius (non-speaking role)

Octavius' party

Octavia – Octavius' sister
Maecenas
Agrippa – admiral of the Roman navy
Taurus – Octavius' lieutenant general
Dolabella
Thidias
Gallus
Proculeius

Sextus' party

Menecrates
Menas
Varrius

Cleopatra's party

    Charmian – maid of honour
    Iras – maid of honour
    Alexas

Mardian – a eunuch
Diomedes – treasurer
Seleucus – attendant

Other

Soothsayer
Clown
Boy
Sentry
Officers, Soldiers, Messengers, Attendants

And now, the Play…

ACT I

SCENE I.
Alexandria. A room in CLEOPATRA's palace.

Enter DEMETRIUS and PHILO

PHILO
  Nay, but this dotage of our general's
  O'erflows the measure: those his goodly eyes,
  That o'er the files and musters of the war
  Have glow'd like plated Mars, now bend, now turn,
  The office and devotion of their view
  Upon a tawny front: his captain's heart,
  Which in the scuffles of great fights hath burst
  The buckles on his breast, reneges all temper,
  And is become the bellows and the fan
  To cool a gipsy's lust.

  Flourish. Enter ANTONY, CLEOPATRA, her Ladies, the Train, with Eunuchs fanning her

  Look, where they come:
  Take but good note, and you shall see in him.
  The triple pillar of the world transform'd
  Into a strumpet's fool: behold and see.
CLEOPATRA
  If it be love indeed, tell me how much.
MARK ANTONY
  There's beggary in the love that can be reckon'd.
CLEOPATRA
  I'll set a bourn how far to be beloved.
MARK ANTONY
  Then must thou needs find out new heaven, new earth.

The Tragedie of Anthonie and Cleopatra— Act I

Enter an Attendant

Attendant
  News, my good lord, from Rome.
MARK ANTONY
  Grates me: the sum.
CLEOPATRA
  Nay, hear them, Antony:
  Fulvia perchance is angry; or, who knows
  If the scarce-bearded Caesar have not sent
  His powerful mandate to you, 'Do this, or this;
  Take in that kingdom, and enfranchise that;
  Perform 't, or else we damn thee.'
MARK ANTONY
  How, my love!
CLEOPATRA
  Perchance! nay, and most like:
  You must not stay here longer, your dismission
  Is come from Caesar; therefore hear it, Antony.
  Where's Fulvia's process? Caesar's I would say? both?
  Call in the messengers. As I am Egypt's queen,
  Thou blushest, Antony; and that blood of thine
  Is Caesar's homager: else so thy cheek pays shame
  When shrill-tongued Fulvia scolds. The messengers!
MARK ANTONY
  Let Rome in Tiber melt, and the wide arch
  Of the ranged empire fall! Here is my space.
  Kingdoms are clay: our dungy earth alike
  Feeds beast as man: the nobleness of life
  Is to do thus; when such a mutual pair

            Embracing
  And such a twain can do't, in which I bind,
  On pain of punishment, the world to weet
  We stand up peerless.

The Tragedie of Anthonie and Cleopatra— Act I

CLEOPATRA
  Excellent falsehood!
  Why did he marry Fulvia, and not love her?
  I'll seem the fool I am not; Antony
  Will be himself.
MARK ANTONY
  But stirr'd by Cleopatra.
  Now, for the love of Love and her soft hours,
  Let's not confound the time with conference harsh:
  There's not a minute of our lives should stretch
  Without some pleasure now. What sport tonight?
CLEOPATRA
  Hear the ambassadors.
MARK ANTONY
  Fie, wrangling queen!
  Whom every thing becomes, to chide, to laugh,
  To weep; whose every passion fully strives
  To make itself, in thee, fair and admired!
  No messenger, but thine; and all alone
  To-night we'll wander through the streets and note
  The qualities of people. Come, my queen;
  Last night you did desire it: speak not to us.

  Exeunt MARK ANTONY and CLEOPATRA with their train

DEMETRIUS
  Is Caesar with Antonius prized so slight?
PHILO
  Sir, sometimes, when he is not Antony,
  He comes too short of that great property
  Which still should go with Antony.
DEMETRIUS
  I am full sorry
  That he approves the common liar, who
  Thus speaks of him at Rome: but I will hope

Of better deeds to-morrow. Rest you happy!

Exeunt

SCENE II.
The same. Another room.

Enter CHARMIAN, IRAS, ALEXAS, and a Soothsayer

CHARMIAN
   Lord Alexas, sweet Alexas, most any thing Alexas,
   almost most absolute Alexas, where's the soothsayer
   that you praised so to the queen? O, that I knew
   this husband, which, you say, must charge his horns
   with garlands!
ALEXAS
   Soothsayer!
Soothsayer
   Your will?
CHARMIAN
   Is this the man? Is't you, sir, that know things?
Soothsayer
   In nature's infinite book of secrecy
   A little I can read.
ALEXAS
   Show him your hand.

Enter DOMITIUS ENOBARBUS

DOMITIUS ENOBARBUS
   Bring in the banquet quickly; wine enough
   Cleopatra's health to drink.
CHARMIAN
   Good sir, give me good fortune.

The Tragedie of Anthonie and Cleopatra— Act I

Soothsayer
  I make not, but foresee.
CHARMIAN
  Pray, then, foresee me one.
Soothsayer
  You shall be yet far fairer than you are.
CHARMIAN
  He means in flesh.
IRAS
  No, you shall paint when you are old.
CHARMIAN
  Wrinkles forbid!
ALEXAS
  Vex not his prescience; be attentive.
CHARMIAN
  Hush!
Soothsayer
  You shall be more beloving than beloved.
CHARMIAN
  I had rather heat my liver with drinking.
ALEXAS
  Nay, hear him.
CHARMIAN
  Good now, some excellent fortune! Let me be married
  to three kings in a forenoon, and widow them all:
  let me have a child at fifty, to whom Herod of Jewry
  may do homage: find me to marry me with Octavius
  Caesar, and companion me with my mistress.
Soothsayer
  You shall outlive the lady whom you serve.
CHARMIAN
  O excellent! I love long life better than figs.
Soothsayer
  You have seen and proved a fairer former fortune

The Tragedie of Anthonie and Cleopatra— Act I

Than that which is to approach.
CHARMIAN
   Then belike my children shall have no names:
   prithee, how many boys and wenches must I have?
Soothsayer
   If every of your wishes had a womb.
   And fertile every wish, a million.
CHARMIAN
   Out, fool! I forgive thee for a witch.
ALEXAS
   You think none but your sheets are privy to your wishes.
CHARMIAN
   Nay, come, tell Iras hers.
ALEXAS
   We'll know all our fortunes.
DOMITIUS ENOBARBUS
   Mine, and most of our fortunes, to-night, shall
   be--drunk to bed.
IRAS
   There's a palm presages chastity, if nothing else.
CHARMIAN
   E'en as the o'erflowing Nilus presageth famine.
IRAS
   Go, you wild bedfellow, you cannot soothsay.
CHARMIAN
   Nay, if an oily palm be not a fruitful
   prognostication, I cannot scratch mine ear. Prithee,
   tell her but a worky-day fortune.
Soothsayer
   Your fortunes are alike.
IRAS
   But how, but how? give me particulars.
Soothsayer
   I have said.

The Tragedie of Anthonie and Cleopatra— Act I

IRAS
Am I not an inch of fortune better than she?
CHARMIAN
Well, if you were but an inch of fortune better than
I, where would you choose it?
IRAS
Not in my husband's nose.
CHARMIAN
Our worser thoughts heavens mend! Alexas,--come,
his fortune, his fortune! O, let him marry a woman
that cannot go, sweet Isis, I beseech thee! and let
her die too, and give him a worse! and let worst
follow worse, till the worst of all follow him
laughing to his grave, fifty-fold a cuckold! Good
Isis, hear me this prayer, though thou deny me a
matter of more weight; good Isis, I beseech thee!
IRAS
Amen. Dear goddess, hear that prayer of the people!
for, as it is a heartbreaking to see a handsome man
loose-wived, so it is a deadly sorrow to behold a
foul knave uncuckolded: therefore, dear Isis, keep
decorum, and fortune him accordingly!
CHARMIAN
Amen.
ALEXAS
Lo, now, if it lay in their hands to make me a
cuckold, they would make themselves whores, but
they'ld do't!
DOMITIUS ENOBARBUS
Hush! here comes Antony.
CHARMIAN
Not he; the queen.

Enter CLEOPATRA

The Tragedie of Anthonie and Cleopatra— Act I

CLEOPATRA
  Saw you my lord?
DOMITIUS ENOBARBUS
  No, lady.
CLEOPATRA
  Was he not here?
CHARMIAN
  No, madam.
CLEOPATRA
  He was disposed to mirth; but on the sudden
  A Roman thought hath struck him. Enobarbus!
DOMITIUS ENOBARBUS
  Madam?
CLEOPATRA
  Seek him, and bring him hither.
  Where's Alexas?
ALEXAS
  Here, at your service. My lord approaches.
CLEOPATRA
  We will not look upon him: go with us.

Exeunt

Enter MARK ANTONY with a Messenger and Attendants

Messenger
  Fulvia thy wife first came into the field.
MARK ANTONY
  Against my brother Lucius?
Messenger
  Ay:
  But soon that war had end, and the time's state
  Made friends of them, joining their force 'gainst Caesar;
  Whose better issue in the war, from Italy,

    Upon the first encounter, drave them.
MARK ANTONY
    Well, what worst?
Messenger
    The nature of bad news infects the teller.
MARK ANTONY
    When it concerns the fool or coward. On:
    Things that are past are done with me. 'Tis thus:
    Who tells me true, though in his tale lie death,
    I hear him as he flatter'd.
Messenger
    Labienus--
    This is stiff news--hath, with his Parthian force,
    Extended Asia from Euphrates;
    His conquering banner shook from Syria
    To Lydia and to Ionia; Whilst--
MARK ANTONY
    Antony, thou wouldst say,--
Messenger
    O, my lord!
MARK ANTONY
    Speak to me home, mince not the general tongue:
    Name Cleopatra as she is call'd in Rome;
    Rail thou in Fulvia's phrase; and taunt my faults
    With such full licence as both truth and malice
    Have power to utter. O, then we bring forth weeds,
    When our quick minds lie still; and our ills told us
    Is as our earing. Fare thee well awhile.
Messenger
    At your noble pleasure.

Exit

MARK ANTONY
    From Sicyon, ho, the news! Speak there!

The Tragedie of Anthonie and Cleopatra— Act I

First Attendant
   The man from Sicyon,--is there such an one?
Second Attendant
   He stays upon your will.
MARK ANTONY
   Let him appear.
   These strong Egyptian fetters I must break,
   Or lose myself in dotage.

Enter another Messenger

   What are you?
Second Messenger
   Fulvia thy wife is dead.
MARK ANTONY
   Where died she?
Second Messenger
   In Sicyon:
   Her length of sickness, with what else more serious
   Importeth thee to know, this bears.

Gives a letter

MARK ANTONY
   Forbear me.

Exit Second Messenger

   There's a great spirit gone! Thus did I desire it:
   What our contempt doth often hurl from us,
   We wish it ours again; the present pleasure,
   By revolution lowering, does become
   The opposite of itself: she's good, being gone;
   The hand could pluck her back that shoved her on.
   I must from this enchanting queen break off:
   Ten thousand harms, more than the ills I know,
   My idleness doth hatch. How now! Enobarbus!

The Tragedie of Anthonie and Cleopatra— Act I

Re-enter DOMITIUS ENOBARBUS

DOMITIUS ENOBARBUS
What's your pleasure, sir?
MARK ANTONY
I must with haste from hence.
DOMITIUS ENOBARBUS
Why, then, we kill all our women:
we see how mortal an unkindness is to them;
if they suffer our departure, death's the word.
MARK ANTONY
I must be gone.
DOMITIUS ENOBARBUS
Under a compelling occasion, let women die; it were
pity to cast them away for nothing; though, between
them and a great cause, they should be esteemed
nothing. Cleopatra, catching but the least noise of
this, dies instantly; I have seen her die twenty
times upon far poorer moment: I do think there is
mettle in death, which commits some loving act upon
her, she hath such a celerity in dying.
MARK ANTONY
She is cunning past man's thought.

Exit ALEXAS

DOMITIUS ENOBARBUS
Alack, sir, no; her passions are made of nothing but
the finest part of pure love: we cannot call her
winds and waters sighs and tears; they are greater
storms and tempests than almanacs can report: this
cannot be cunning in her; if it be, she makes a
shower of rain as well as Jove.
MARK ANTONY
Would I had never seen her.

The Tragedie of Anthonie and Cleopatra— Act I

DOMITIUS ENOBARBUS
O, sir, you had then left unseen a wonderful piece of work; which not to have been blest withal would have discredited your travel.

MARK ANTONY
Fulvia is dead.

DOMITIUS ENOBARBUS
Sir?

MARK ANTONY
Fulvia is dead.

DOMITIUS ENOBARBUS
Fulvia!

MARK ANTONY
Dead.

DOMITIUS ENOBARBUS
Why, sir, give the gods a thankful sacrifice. When it pleaseth their deities to take the wife of a man from him, it shows to man the tailors of the earth; comforting therein, that when old robes are worn out, there are members to make new. If there were no more women but Fulvia, then had you indeed a cut, and the case to be lamented: this grief is crowned with consolation; your old smock brings forth a new petticoat: and indeed the tears live in an onion that should water this sorrow.

MARK ANTONY
The business she hath broached in the state
Cannot endure my absence.

DOMITIUS ENOBARBUS
And the business you have broached here cannot be without you; especially that of Cleopatra's, which wholly depends on your abode.

MARK ANTONY
No more light answers. Let our officers

The Tragedie of Anthonie and Cleopatra— Act I

Have notice what we purpose. I shall break
The cause of our expedience to the queen,
And get her leave to part. For not alone
The death of Fulvia, with more urgent touches,
Do strongly speak to us; but the letters too
Of many our contriving friends in Rome
Petition us at home: Sextus Pompeius
Hath given the dare to Caesar, and commands
The empire of the sea: our slippery people,
Whose love is never link'd to the deserver
Till his deserts are past, begin to throw
Pompey the Great and all his dignities
Upon his son; who, high in name and power,
Higher than both in blood and life, stands up
For the main soldier: whose quality, going on,
The sides o' the world may danger: much is breeding,
Which, like the courser's hair, hath yet but life,
And not a serpent's poison. Say, our pleasure,
To such whose place is under us, requires
Our quick remove from hence.

DOMITIUS ENOBARBUS
I shall do't.

Exeunt

SCENE III.
The same. Another room.

Enter CLEOPATRA, CHARMIAN, IRAS, and ALEXAS

CLEOPATRA
  Where is he?
CHARMIAN
  I did not see him since.
CLEOPATRA
  See where he is, who's with him, what he does:
  I did not send you: if you find him sad,
  Say I am dancing; if in mirth, report
  That I am sudden sick: quick, and return.

           Exit ALEXAS

CHARMIAN
  Madam, methinks, if you did love him dearly,
  You do not hold the method to enforce
  The like from him.
CLEOPATRA
  What should I do, I do not?
CHARMIAN
  In each thing give him way, cross him nothing.
CLEOPATRA
  Thou teachest like a fool; the way to lose him.
CHARMIAN
  Tempt him not so too far; I wish, forbear:
  In time we hate that which we often fear.
  But here comes Antony.

         Enter MARK ANTONY

CLEOPATRA
  I am sick and sullen.

The Tragedie of Anthonie and Cleopatra— Act I

MARK ANTONY
I am sorry to give breathing to my purpose,--
CLEOPATRA
Help me away, dear Charmian; I shall fall:
It cannot be thus long, the sides of nature
Will not sustain it.
MARK ANTONY
Now, my dearest queen,--
CLEOPATRA
Pray you, stand further from me.
MARK ANTONY
What's the matter?
CLEOPATRA
I know, by that same eye, there's some good news.
What says the married woman? You may go:
Would she had never given you leave to come!
Let her not say 'tis I that keep you here:
I have no power upon you; hers you are.
MARK ANTONY
The gods best know,--
CLEOPATRA
O, never was there queen
So mightily betray'd! yet at the first
I saw the treasons planted.
MARK ANTONY
Cleopatra,--
CLEOPATRA
Why should I think you can be mine and true,
Though you in swearing shake the throned gods,
Who have been false to Fulvia? Riotous madness,
To be entangled with those mouth-made vows,
Which break themselves in swearing!
MARK ANTONY
Most sweet queen,--

The Tragedie of Anthonie and Cleopatra— Act I

CLEOPATRA
  Nay, pray you, seek no colour for your going,
  But bid farewell, and go: when you sued staying,
  Then was the time for words: no going then;
  Eternity was in our lips and eyes,
  Bliss in our brows' bent; none our parts so poor,
  But was a race of heaven: they are so still,
  Or thou, the greatest soldier of the world,
  Art turn'd the greatest liar.
MARK ANTONY
  How now, lady!
CLEOPATRA
  I would I had thy inches; thou shouldst know
  There were a heart in Egypt.
MARK ANTONY
  Hear me, queen:
  The strong necessity of time commands
  Our services awhile; but my full heart
  Remains in use with you. Our Italy
  Shines o'er with civil swords: Sextus Pompeius
  Makes his approaches to the port of Rome:
  Equality of two domestic powers
  Breed scrupulous faction: the hated, grown to strength,
  Are newly grown to love: the condemn'd Pompey,
  Rich in his father's honour, creeps apace,
  Into the hearts of such as have not thrived
  Upon the present state, whose numbers threaten;
  And quietness, grown sick of rest, would purge
  By any desperate change: my more particular,
  And that which most with you should safe my going,
  Is Fulvia's death.
CLEOPATRA
  Though age from folly could not give me freedom,
  It does from childishness: can Fulvia die?

The Tragedie of Anthonie and Cleopatra— Act I

MARK ANTONY
  She's dead, my queen:
  Look here, and at thy sovereign leisure read
  The garboils she awaked; at the last, best:
  See when and where she died.

CLEOPATRA
  O most false love!
  Where be the sacred vials thou shouldst fill
  With sorrowful water? Now I see, I see,
  In Fulvia's death, how mine received shall be.

MARK ANTONY
  Quarrel no more, but be prepared to know
  The purposes I bear; which are, or cease,
  As you shall give the advice. By the fire
  That quickens Nilus' slime, I go from hence
  Thy soldier, servant; making peace or war
  As thou affect'st.

CLEOPATRA
  Cut my lace, Charmian, come;
  But let it be: I am quickly ill, and well,
  So Antony loves.

MARK ANTONY
  My precious queen, forbear;
  And give true evidence to his love, which stands
  An honourable trial.

CLEOPATRA
  So Fulvia told me.
  I prithee, turn aside and weep for her,
  Then bid adieu to me, and say the tears
  Belong to Egypt: good now, play one scene
  Of excellent dissembling; and let it look
  Life perfect honour.

MARK ANTONY
  You'll heat my blood: no more.

CLEOPATRA
  You can do better yet; but this is meetly.
MARK ANTONY
  Now, by my sword,--
CLEOPATRA
  And target. Still he mends;
  But this is not the best. Look, prithee, Charmian,
  How this Herculean Roman does become
  The carriage of his chafe.
MARK ANTONY
  I'll leave you, lady.
CLEOPATRA
  Courteous lord, one word.
  Sir, you and I must part, but that's not it:
  Sir, you and I have loved, but there's not it;
  That you know well: something it is I would,
  O, my oblivion is a very Antony,
  And I am all forgotten.
MARK ANTONY
  But that your royalty
  Holds idleness your subject, I should take you
  For idleness itself.
CLEOPATRA
  'Tis sweating labour
  To bear such idleness so near the heart
  As Cleopatra this. But, sir, forgive me;
  Since my becomings kill me, when they do not
  Eye well to you: your honour calls you hence;
  Therefore be deaf to my unpitied folly.
  And all the gods go with you! upon your sword
  Sit laurel victory! and smooth success
  Be strew'd before your feet!
MARK ANTONY
  Let us go. Come;

The Tragedie of Anthonie and Cleopatra— Act I

Our separation so abides, and flies,
That thou, residing here, go'st yet with me,
And I, hence fleeting, here remain with thee. Away!

Exeunt

SCENE IV.
Rome. OCTAVIUS CAESAR's house.

Enter OCTAVIUS CAESAR, reading a letter, LEPIDUS, and their Train

OCTAVIUS CAESAR
  You may see, Lepidus, and henceforth know,
  It is not Caesar's natural vice to hate
  Our great competitor: from Alexandria
  This is the news: he fishes, drinks, and wastes
  The lamps of night in revel; is not more man-like
  Than Cleopatra; nor the queen of Ptolemy
  More womanly than he; hardly gave audience, or
  Vouchsafed to think he had partners: you shall find there
  A man who is the abstract of all faults
  That all men follow.
LEPIDUS
  I must not think there are
  Evils enow to darken all his goodness:
  His faults in him seem as the spots of heaven,
  More fiery by night's blackness; hereditary,
  Rather than purchased; what he cannot change,
  Than what he chooses.
OCTAVIUS CAESAR
  You are too indulgent. Let us grant, it is not
  Amiss to tumble on the bed of Ptolemy;
  To give a kingdom for a mirth; to sit

The Tragedie of Anthonie and Cleopatra— Act I

And keep the turn of tippling with a slave;
To reel the streets at noon, and stand the buffet
With knaves that smell of sweat: say this
becomes him,--
As his composure must be rare indeed
Whom these things cannot blemish,--yet must Antony
No way excuse his soils, when we do bear
So great weight in his lightness. If he fill'd
His vacancy with his voluptuousness,
Full surfeits, and the dryness of his bones,
Call on him for't: but to confound such time,
That drums him from his sport, and speaks as loud
As his own state and ours,--'tis to be chid
As we rate boys, who, being mature in knowledge,
Pawn their experience to their present pleasure,
And so rebel to judgment.

Enter a Messenger

LEPIDUS
  Here's more news.
Messenger
  Thy biddings have been done; and every hour,
  Most noble Caesar, shalt thou have report
  How 'tis abroad. Pompey is strong at sea;
  And it appears he is beloved of those
  That only have fear'd Caesar: to the ports
  The discontents repair, and men's reports
  Give him much wrong'd.
OCTAVIUS CAESAR
  I should have known no less.
  It hath been taught us from the primal state,
  That he which is was wish'd until he were;
  And the ebb'd man, ne'er loved till ne'er worth love,
  Comes dear'd by being lack'd. This common body,

    Like to a vagabond flag upon the stream,
    Goes to and back, lackeying the varying tide,
    To rot itself with motion.
Messenger
    Caesar, I bring thee word,
    Menecrates and Menas, famous pirates,
    Make the sea serve them, which they ear and wound
    With keels of every kind: many hot inroads
    They make in Italy; the borders maritime
    Lack blood to think on't, and flush youth revolt:
    No vessel can peep forth, but 'tis as soon
    Taken as seen; for Pompey's name strikes more
    Than could his war resisted.
OCTAVIUS CAESAR
    Antony,
    Leave thy lascivious wassails. When thou once
    Wast beaten from Modena, where thou slew'st
    Hirtius and Pansa, consuls, at thy heel
    Did famine follow; whom thou fought'st against,
    Though daintily brought up, with patience more
    Than savages could suffer: thou didst drink
    The stale of horses, and the gilded puddle
    Which beasts would cough at: thy palate then did deign
    The roughest berry on the rudest hedge;
    Yea, like the stag, when snow the pasture sheets,
    The barks of trees thou browsed'st; on the Alps
    It is reported thou didst eat strange flesh,
    Which some did die to look on: and all this--
    It wounds thine honour that I speak it now--
    Was borne so like a soldier, that thy cheek
    So much as lank'd not.
LEPIDUS
    'Tis pity of him.

OCTAVIUS CAESAR
  Let his shames quickly
  Drive him to Rome: 'tis time we twain
  Did show ourselves i' the field; and to that end
  Assemble we immediate council: Pompey
  Thrives in our idleness.
LEPIDUS
  To-morrow, Caesar,
  I shall be furnish'd to inform you rightly
  Both what by sea and land I can be able
  To front this present time.
OCTAVIUS CAESAR
  Till which encounter,
  It is my business too. Farewell.
LEPIDUS
  Farewell, my lord: what you shall know meantime
  Of stirs abroad, I shall beseech you, sir,
  To let me be partaker.
OCTAVIUS CAESAR
  Doubt not, sir;
  I knew it for my bond.

Exeunt

SCENE V.
Alexandria. CLEOPATRA's palace.

Enter CLEOPATRA, CHARMIAN, IRAS, and MARDIAN

CLEOPATRA
  Charmian!
CHARMIAN
  Madam?

The Tragedie of Anthonie and Cleopatra— Act I

CLEOPATRA
　Ha, ha!
　Give me to drink mandragora.
CHARMIAN
　Why, madam?
CLEOPATRA
　That I might sleep out this great gap of time
　My Antony is away.
CHARMIAN
　You think of him too much.
CLEOPATRA
　O, 'tis treason!
CHARMIAN
　Madam, I trust, not so.
CLEOPATRA
　Thou, eunuch Mardian!
MARDIAN
　What's your highness' pleasure?
CLEOPATRA
　Not now to hear thee sing; I take no pleasure
　In aught an eunuch has: 'tis well for thee,
　That, being unseminar'd, thy freer thoughts
　May not fly forth of Egypt. Hast thou affections?
MARDIAN
　Yes, gracious madam.
CLEOPATRA
　Indeed!
MARDIAN
　Not in deed, madam; for I can do nothing
　But what indeed is honest to be done:
　Yet have I fierce affections, and think
　What Venus did with Mars.
CLEOPATRA
　O Charmian,

The Tragedie of Anthonie and Cleopatra— Act I

Where think'st thou he is now? Stands he, or sits he?
Or does he walk? or is he on his horse?
O happy horse, to bear the weight of Antony!
Do bravely, horse! for wot'st thou whom thou movest?
The demi-Atlas of this earth, the arm
And burgonet of men. He's speaking now,
Or murmuring 'Where's my serpent of old Nile?'
For so he calls me: now I feed myself
With most delicious poison. Think on me,
That am with Phoebus' amorous pinches black,
And wrinkled deep in time? Broad-fronted Caesar,
When thou wast here above the ground, I was
A morsel for a monarch: and great Pompey
Would stand and make his eyes grow in my brow;
There would he anchor his aspect and die
With looking on his life.

Enter ALEXAS, from OCTAVIUS CAESAR

ALEXAS
 Sovereign of Egypt, hail!
CLEOPATRA
 How much unlike art thou Mark Antony!
 Yet, coming from him, that great medicine hath
 With his tinct gilded thee.
 How goes it with my brave Mark Antony?
ALEXAS
 Last thing he did, dear queen,
 He kiss'd,--the last of many doubled kisses,--
 This orient pearl. His speech sticks in my heart.
CLEOPATRA
 Mine ear must pluck it thence.
ALEXAS
 'Good friend,' quoth he,
 'Say, the firm Roman to great Egypt sends

This treasure of an oyster; at whose foot,
To mend the petty present, I will piece
Her opulent throne with kingdoms; all the east,
Say thou, shall call her mistress.' So he nodded,
And soberly did mount an arm-gaunt steed,
Who neigh'd so high, that what I would have spoke
Was beastly dumb'd by him.

CLEOPATRA
What, was he sad or merry?

ALEXAS
Like to the time o' the year between the extremes
Of hot and cold, he was nor sad nor merry.

CLEOPATRA
O well-divided disposition! Note him,
Note him good Charmian, 'tis the man; but note him:
He was not sad, for he would shine on those
That make their looks by his; he was not merry,
Which seem'd to tell them his remembrance lay
In Egypt with his joy; but between both:
O heavenly mingle! Be'st thou sad or merry,
The violence of either thee becomes,
So does it no man else. Met'st thou my posts?

ALEXAS
Ay, madam, twenty several messengers:
Why do you send so thick?

CLEOPATRA
Who's born that day
When I forget to send to Antony,
Shall die a beggar. Ink and paper, Charmian.
Welcome, my good Alexas. Did I, Charmian,
Ever love Caesar so?

CHARMIAN
O that brave Caesar!

CLEOPATRA
  Be choked with such another emphasis!
  Say, the brave Antony.
CHARMIAN
  The valiant Caesar!
CLEOPATRA
  By Isis, I will give thee bloody teeth,
  If thou with Caesar paragon again
  My man of men.
CHARMIAN
  By your most gracious pardon,
  I sing but after you.
CLEOPATRA
  My salad days,
  When I was green in judgment: cold in blood,
  To say as I said then! But, come, away;
  Get me ink and paper:
  He shall have every day a several greeting,
  Or I'll unpeople Egypt.

Exeunt

ACT II

SCENE I.
Messina. POMPEY's house.

Enter POMPEY, MENECRATES, and MENAS, in warlike manner

POMPEY
If the great gods be just, they shall assist
The deeds of justest men.
MENECRATES
Know, worthy Pompey,
That what they do delay, they not deny.
POMPEY
Whiles we are suitors to their throne, decays
The thing we sue for.
MENECRATES
We, ignorant of ourselves,
Beg often our own harms, which the wise powers
Deny us for our good; so find we profit
By losing of our prayers.
POMPEY
I shall do well:
The people love me, and the sea is mine;
My powers are crescent, and my auguring hope
Says it will come to the full. Mark Antony
In Egypt sits at dinner, and will make
No wars without doors: Caesar gets money where
He loses hearts: Lepidus flatters both,
Of both is flatter'd; but he neither loves,
Nor either cares for him.
MENAS
Caesar and Lepidus

    Are in the field: a mighty strength they carry.
POMPEY
    Where have you this? 'tis false.
MENAS
    From Silvius, sir.
POMPEY
    He dreams: I know they are in Rome together,
    Looking for Antony. But all the charms of love,
    Salt Cleopatra, soften thy waned lip!
    Let witchcraft join with beauty, lust with both!
    Tie up the libertine in a field of feasts,
    Keep his brain fuming; Epicurean cooks
    Sharpen with cloyless sauce his appetite;
    That sleep and feeding may prorogue his honour
    Even till a Lethe'd dulness!

Enter VARRIUS

    How now, Varrius!
VARRIUS
    This is most certain that I shall deliver:
    Mark Antony is every hour in Rome
    Expected: since he went from Egypt 'tis
    A space for further travel.
POMPEY
    I could have given less matter
    A better ear. Menas, I did not think
    This amorous surfeiter would have donn'd his helm
    For such a petty war: his soldiership
    Is twice the other twain: but let us rear
    The higher our opinion, that our stirring
    Can from the lap of Egypt's widow pluck
    The ne'er-lust-wearied Antony.
MENAS
    I cannot hope
    Caesar and Antony shall well greet together:

His wife that's dead did trespasses to Caesar;
His brother warr'd upon him; although, I think,
Not moved by Antony.
POMPEY
I know not, Menas,
How lesser enmities may give way to greater.
Were't not that we stand up against them all,
'Twere pregnant they should square between themselves;
For they have entertained cause enough
To draw their swords: but how the fear of us
May cement their divisions and bind up
The petty difference, we yet not know.
Be't as our gods will have't! It only stands
Our lives upon to use our strongest hands.
Come, Menas.

Exeunt

SCENE II.
Rome. The house of LEPIDUS.

Enter DOMITIUS ENOBARBUS and LEPIDUS

LEPIDUS
Good Enobarbus, 'tis a worthy deed,
And shall become you well, to entreat your captain
To soft and gentle speech.
DOMITIUS ENOBARBUS
I shall entreat him
To answer like himself: if Caesar move him,
Let Antony look over Caesar's head
And speak as loud as Mars. By Jupiter,
Were I the wearer of Antonius' beard,

The Tragedie of Anthonie and Cleopatra — Act II

    I would not shave't to-day.
LEPIDUS
    'Tis not a time
    For private stomaching.
DOMITIUS ENOBARBUS
    Every time
    Serves for the matter that is then born in't.
LEPIDUS
    But small to greater matters must give way.
DOMITIUS ENOBARBUS
    Not if the small come first.
LEPIDUS
    Your speech is passion:
    But, pray you, stir no embers up. Here comes
    The noble Antony.

        Enter MARK ANTONY and VENTIDIUS

DOMITIUS ENOBARBUS
    And yonder, Caesar.

        Enter OCTAVIUS CAESAR, MECAENAS, and AGRIPPA

MARK ANTONY
    If we compose well here, to Parthia:
    Hark, Ventidius.
OCTAVIUS CAESAR
    I do not know,
    Mecaenas; ask Agrippa.
LEPIDUS
    Noble friends,
    That which combined us was most great, and let not
    A leaner action rend us. What's amiss,
    May it be gently heard: when we debate
    Our trivial difference loud, we do commit

Murder in healing wounds: then, noble partners,
The rather, for I earnestly beseech,
Touch you the sourest points with sweetest terms,
Nor curstness grow to the matter.
MARK ANTONY
'Tis spoken well.
Were we before our armies, and to fight.
I should do thus.

Flourish

OCTAVIUS CAESAR
Welcome to Rome.
MARK ANTONY
Thank you.
OCTAVIUS CAESAR
Sit.
MARK ANTONY
Sit, sir.
OCTAVIUS CAESAR
Nay, then.
MARK ANTONY
I learn, you take things ill which are not so,
Or being, concern you not.
OCTAVIUS CAESAR
I must be laugh'd at,
If, or for nothing or a little, I
Should say myself offended, and with you
Chiefly i' the world; more laugh'd at, that I should
Once name you derogately, when to sound your name
It not concern'd me.
MARK ANTONY
My being in Egypt, Caesar,
What was't to you?

OCTAVIUS CAESAR
  No more than my residing here at Rome
  Might be to you in Egypt: yet, if you there
  Did practise on my state, your being in Egypt
  Might be my question.
MARK ANTONY
  How intend you, practised?
OCTAVIUS CAESAR
  You may be pleased to catch at mine intent
  By what did here befal me. Your wife and brother
  Made wars upon me; and their contestation
  Was theme for you, you were the word of war.
MARK ANTONY
  You do mistake your business; my brother never
  Did urge me in his act: I did inquire it;
  And have my learning from some true reports,
  That drew their swords with you. Did he not rather
  Discredit my authority with yours;
  And make the wars alike against my stomach,
  Having alike your cause? Of this my letters
  Before did satisfy you. If you'll patch a quarrel,
  As matter whole you have not to make it with,
  It must not be with this.
OCTAVIUS CAESAR
  You praise yourself
  By laying defects of judgment to me; but
  You patch'd up your excuses.
MARK ANTONY
  Not so, not so;
  I know you could not lack, I am certain on't,
  Very necessity of this thought, that I,
  Your partner in the cause 'gainst which he fought,
  Could not with graceful eyes attend those wars
  Which fronted mine own peace. As for my wife,

I would you had her spirit in such another:
The third o' the world is yours; which with a snaffle
You may pace easy, but not such a wife.
DOMITIUS ENOBARBUS
Would we had all such wives, that the men might go
to wars with the women!
MARK ANTONY
So much uncurbable, her garboils, Caesar
Made out of her impatience, which not wanted
Shrewdness of policy too, I grieving grant
Did you too much disquiet: for that you must
But say, I could not help it.
OCTAVIUS CAESAR
I wrote to you
When rioting in Alexandria; you
Did pocket up my letters, and with taunts
Did gibe my missive out of audience.
MARK ANTONY
Sir,
He fell upon me ere admitted: then
Three kings I had newly feasted, and did want
Of what I was i' the morning: but next day
I told him of myself; which was as much
As to have ask'd him pardon. Let this fellow
Be nothing of our strife; if we contend,
Out of our question wipe him.
OCTAVIUS CAESAR
You have broken
The article of your oath; which you shall never
Have tongue to charge me with.
LEPIDUS
Soft, Caesar!
MARK ANTONY
No,

Lepidus, let him speak:
The honour is sacred which he talks on now,
Supposing that I lack'd it. But, on, Caesar;
The article of my oath.

OCTAVIUS CAESAR
To lend me arms and aid when I required them;
The which you both denied.

MARK ANTONY
Neglected, rather;
And then when poison'd hours had bound me up
From mine own knowledge. As nearly as I may,
I'll play the penitent to you: but mine honesty
Shall not make poor my greatness, nor my power
Work without it. Truth is, that Fulvia,
To have me out of Egypt, made wars here;
For which myself, the ignorant motive, do
So far ask pardon as befits mine honour
To stoop in such a case.

LEPIDUS
'Tis noble spoken.

MECAENAS
If it might please you, to enforce no further
The griefs between ye: to forget them quite
Were to remember that the present need
Speaks to atone you.

LEPIDUS
Worthily spoken, Mecaenas.

DOMITIUS ENOBARBUS
Or, if you borrow one another's love for the
instant, you may, when you hear no more words of
Pompey, return it again: you shall have time to
wrangle in when you have nothing else to do.

MARK ANTONY
Thou art a soldier only: speak no more.

DOMITIUS ENOBARBUS
  That truth should be silent I had almost forgot.
MARK ANTONY
  You wrong this presence; therefore speak no more.
DOMITIUS ENOBARBUS
  Go to, then; your considerate stone.
OCTAVIUS CAESAR
  I do not much dislike the matter, but
  The manner of his speech; for't cannot be
  We shall remain in friendship, our conditions
  So differing in their acts. Yet if I knew
  What hoop should hold us stanch, from edge to edge
  O' the world I would pursue it.
AGRIPPA
  Give me leave, Caesar,--
OCTAVIUS CAESAR
  Speak, Agrippa.
AGRIPPA
  Thou hast a sister by the mother's side,
  Admired Octavia: great Mark Antony
  Is now a widower.
OCTAVIUS CAESAR
  Say not so, Agrippa:
  If Cleopatra heard you, your reproof
  Were well deserved of rashness.
MARK ANTONY
  I am not married, Caesar: let me hear
  Agrippa further speak.
AGRIPPA
  To hold you in perpetual amity,
  To make you brothers, and to knit your hearts
  With an unslipping knot, take Antony
  Octavia to his wife; whose beauty claims
  No worse a husband than the best of men;

    Whose virtue and whose general graces speak
    That which none else can utter. By this marriage,
    All little jealousies, which now seem great,
    And all great fears, which now import their dangers,
    Would then be nothing: truths would be tales,
    Where now half tales be truths: her love to both
    Would, each to other and all loves to both,
    Draw after her. Pardon what I have spoke;
    For 'tis a studied, not a present thought,
    By duty ruminated.

MARK ANTONY
    Will Caesar speak?

OCTAVIUS CAESAR
    Not till he hears how Antony is touch'd
    With what is spoke already.

MARK ANTONY
    What power is in Agrippa,
    If I would say, 'Agrippa, be it so,'
    To make this good?

OCTAVIUS CAESAR
    The power of Caesar, and
    His power unto Octavia.

MARK ANTONY
    May I never
    To this good purpose, that so fairly shows,
    Dream of impediment! Let me have thy hand:
    Further this act of grace: and from this hour
    The heart of brothers govern in our loves
    And sway our great designs!

OCTAVIUS CAESAR
    There is my hand.
    A sister I bequeath you, whom no brother
    Did ever love so dearly: let her live
    To join our kingdoms and our hearts; and never

   Fly off our loves again!
LEPIDUS
   Happily, amen!
MARK ANTONY
   I did not think to draw my sword 'gainst Pompey;
   For he hath laid strange courtesies and great
   Of late upon me: I must thank him only,
   Lest my remembrance suffer ill report;
   At heel of that, defy him.
LEPIDUS
   Time calls upon's:
   Of us must Pompey presently be sought,
   Or else he seeks out us.
MARK ANTONY
   Where lies he?
OCTAVIUS CAESAR
   About the mount Misenum.
MARK ANTONY
   What is his strength by land?
OCTAVIUS CAESAR
   Great and increasing: but by sea
   He is an absolute master.
MARK ANTONY
   So is the fame.
   Would we had spoke together! Haste we for it:
   Yet, ere we put ourselves in arms, dispatch we
   The business we have talk'd of.
OCTAVIUS CAESAR
   With most gladness:
   And do invite you to my sister's view,
   Whither straight I'll lead you.
MARK ANTONY
   Let us, Lepidus,
   Not lack your company.

LEPIDUS
Noble Antony,
Not sickness should detain me.

Flourish. Exeunt OCTAVIUS CAESAR, MARK ANTONY, and LEPIDUS

MECAENAS
Welcome from Egypt, sir.
DOMITIUS ENOBARBUS
Half the heart of Caesar, worthy Mecaenas! My honourable friend, Agrippa!
AGRIPPA
Good Enobarbus!
MECAENAS
We have cause to be glad that matters are so well digested. You stayed well by 't in Egypt.
DOMITIUS ENOBARBUS
Ay, sir; we did sleep day out of countenance, and made the night light with drinking.
MECAENAS
Eight wild-boars roasted whole at a breakfast, and but twelve persons there; is this true?
DOMITIUS ENOBARBUS
This was but as a fly by an eagle: we had much more monstrous matter of feast, which worthily deserved noting.
MECAENAS
She's a most triumphant lady, if report be square to her.
DOMITIUS ENOBARBUS
When she first met Mark Antony, she pursed up his heart, upon the river of Cydnus.
AGRIPPA
There she appeared indeed; or my reporter devised well for her.

The Tragedie of Anthonie and Cleopatra — Act II

DOMITIUS ENOBARBUS
I will tell you.
The barge she sat in, like a burnish'd throne,
Burn'd on the water: the poop was beaten gold;
Purple the sails, and so perfumed that
The winds were love-sick with them; the oars were silver,
Which to the tune of flutes kept stroke, and made
The water which they beat to follow faster,
As amorous of their strokes. For her own person,
It beggar'd all description: she did lie
In her pavilion--cloth-of-gold of tissue--
O'er-picturing that Venus where we see
The fancy outwork nature: on each side her
Stood pretty dimpled boys, like smiling Cupids,
With divers-colour'd fans, whose wind did seem
To glow the delicate cheeks which they did cool,
And what they undid did.

AGRIPPA
O, rare for Antony!

DOMITIUS ENOBARBUS
Her gentlewomen, like the Nereides,
So many mermaids, tended her i' the eyes,
And made their bends adornings: at the helm
A seeming mermaid steers: the silken tackle
Swell with the touches of those flower-soft hands,
That yarely frame the office. From the barge
A strange invisible perfume hits the sense
Of the adjacent wharfs. The city cast
Her people out upon her; and Antony,
Enthroned i' the market-place, did sit alone,
Whistling to the air; which, but for vacancy,
Had gone to gaze on Cleopatra too,
And made a gap in nature.

AGRIPPA
  Rare Egyptian!
DOMITIUS ENOBARBUS
  Upon her landing, Antony sent to her,
  Invited her to supper: she replied,
  It should be better he became her guest;
  Which she entreated: our courteous Antony,
  Whom ne'er the word of 'No' woman heard speak,
  Being barber'd ten times o'er, goes to the feast,
  And for his ordinary pays his heart
  For what his eyes eat only.
AGRIPPA
  Royal wench!
  She made great Caesar lay his sword to bed:
  He plough'd her, and she cropp'd.
DOMITIUS ENOBARBUS
  I saw her once
  Hop forty paces through the public street;
  And having lost her breath, she spoke, and panted,
  That she did make defect perfection,
  And, breathless, power breathe forth.
MECAENAS
  Now Antony must leave her utterly.
DOMITIUS ENOBARBUS
  Never; he will not:
  Age cannot wither her, nor custom stale
  Her infinite variety: other women cloy
  The appetites they feed: but she makes hungry
  Where most she satisfies; for vilest things
  Become themselves in her: that the holy priests
  Bless her when she is riggish.
MECAENAS
  If beauty, wisdom, modesty, can settle
  The heart of Antony, Octavia is

A blessed lottery to him.
AGRIPPA
Let us go.
Good Enobarbus, make yourself my guest
Whilst you abide here.
DOMITIUS ENOBARBUS
Humbly, sir, I thank you.

Exeunt

SCENE III.
The same. OCTAVIUS CAESAR's house.

Enter MARK ANTONY, OCTAVIUS CAESAR, OCTAVIA between them, and Attendants

MARK ANTONY
The world and my great office will sometimes
Divide me from your bosom.
OCTAVIA
All which time
Before the gods my knee shall bow my prayers
To them for you.
MARK ANTONY
Good night, sir. My Octavia,
Read not my blemishes in the world's report:
I have not kept my square; but that to come
Shall all be done by the rule. Good night, dear lady.
Good night, sir.
OCTAVIUS CAESAR
Good night.

Exeunt OCTAVIUS CAESAR and OCTAVIA

Enter Soothsayer

MARK ANTONY
   Now, sirrah; you do wish yourself in Egypt?
Soothsayer
   Would I had never come from thence, nor you Thither!
MARK ANTONY
   If you can, your reason?
Soothsayer
   I see it in
   My motion, have it not in my tongue: but yet
   Hie you to Egypt again.
MARK ANTONY
   Say to me,
   Whose fortunes shall rise higher, Caesar's or mine?
Soothsayer
   Caesar's.
   Therefore, O Antony, stay not by his side:
   Thy demon, that's thy spirit which keeps thee, is
   Noble, courageous high, unmatchable,
   Where Caesar's is not; but, near him, thy angel
   Becomes a fear, as being o'erpower'd: therefore
   Make space enough between you.
MARK ANTONY
   Speak this no more.
Soothsayer
   To none but thee; no more, but when to thee.
   If thou dost play with him at any game,
   Thou art sure to lose; and, of that natural luck,
   He beats thee 'gainst the odds: thy lustre thickens,
   When he shines by: I say again, thy spirit
   Is all afraid to govern thee near him;
   But, he away, 'tis noble.
MARK ANTONY
   Get thee gone:
   Say to Ventidius I would speak with him:

Exit Soothsayer
He shall to Parthia. Be it art or hap,
He hath spoken true: the very dice obey him;
And in our sports my better cunning faints
Under his chance: if we draw lots, he speeds;
His cocks do win the battle still of mine,
When it is all to nought; and his quails ever
Beat mine, inhoop'd, at odds. I will to Egypt:
And though I make this marriage for my peace,
I' the east my pleasure lies.

Enter VENTIDIUS

O, come, Ventidius,
You must to Parthia: your commission's ready;
Follow me, and receive't.

Exeunt

SCENE IV.
The same. A street.

Enter LEPIDUS, MECAENAS, and AGRIPPA

LEPIDUS
   Trouble yourselves no further: pray you, hasten
   Your generals after.
AGRIPPA
   Sir, Mark Antony
   Will e'en but kiss Octavia, and we'll follow.
LEPIDUS
   Till I shall see you in your soldier's dress,
   Which will become you both, farewell.
MECAENAS
   We shall,

As I conceive the journey, be at the Mount
Before you, Lepidus.
LEPIDUS
Your way is shorter;
My purposes do draw me much about:
You'll win two days upon me.
MECAENAS AGRIPPA
Sir, good success!
LEPIDUS
Farewell.

Exeunt

SCENE V.
Alexandria. CLEOPATRA's palace.

Enter CLEOPATRA, CHARMIAN, IRAS, and ALEXAS

CLEOPATRA
Give me some music; music, moody food
Of us that trade in love.
Attendants
The music, ho!

Enter MARDIAN

CLEOPATRA
Let it alone; let's to billiards: come, Charmian.
CHARMIAN
My arm is sore; best play with Mardian.
CLEOPATRA
As well a woman with an eunuch play'd
As with a woman. Come, you'll play with me, sir?
MARDIAN
As well as I can, madam.

The Tragedie of Anthonie and Cleopatra — Act II

CLEOPATRA
  And when good will is show'd, though't come too short,
  The actor may plead pardon. I'll none now:
  Give me mine angle; we'll to the river: there,
  My music playing far off, I will betray
  Tawny-finn'd fishes; my bended hook shall pierce
  Their slimy jaws; and, as I draw them up,
  I'll think them every one an Antony,
  And say 'Ah, ha! you're caught.'

CHARMIAN
  'Twas merry when
  You wager'd on your angling; when your diver
  Did hang a salt-fish on his hook, which he
  With fervency drew up.

CLEOPATRA
  That time,--O times!--
  I laugh'd him out of patience; and that night
  I laugh'd him into patience; and next morn,
  Ere the ninth hour, I drunk him to his bed;
  Then put my tires and mantles on him, whilst
  I wore his sword Philippan.

                Enter a Messenger

  O, from Italy
  Ram thou thy fruitful tidings in mine ears,
  That long time have been barren.

Messenger
  Madam, madam,--

CLEOPATRA
  Antonius dead!--If thou say so, villain,
  Thou kill'st thy mistress: but well and free,
  If thou so yield him, there is gold, and here
  My bluest veins to kiss; a hand that kings

Have lipp'd, and trembled kissing.
Messenger
   First, madam, he is well.
CLEOPATRA
   Why, there's more gold.
   But, sirrah, mark, we use
   To say the dead are well: bring it to that,
   The gold I give thee will I melt and pour
   Down thy ill-uttering throat.
Messenger
   Good madam, hear me.
CLEOPATRA
   Well, go to, I will;
   But there's no goodness in thy face: if Antony
   Be free and healthful,--so tart a favour
   To trumpet such good tidings! If not well,
   Thou shouldst come like a Fury crown'd with snakes,
   Not like a formal man.
Messenger
   Will't please you hear me?
CLEOPATRA
   I have a mind to strike thee ere thou speak'st:
   Yet if thou say Antony lives, is well,
   Or friends with Caesar, or not captive to him,
   I'll set thee in a shower of gold, and hail
   Rich pearls upon thee.
Messenger
   Madam, he's well.
CLEOPATRA
   Well said.
Messenger
   And friends with Caesar.
CLEOPATRA
   Thou'rt an honest man.

Messenger
   Caesar and he are greater friends than ever.
CLEOPATRA
   Make thee a fortune from me.
Messenger
   But yet, madam,--
CLEOPATRA
   I do not like 'But yet,' it does allay
   The good precedence; fie upon 'But yet'!
   'But yet' is as a gaoler to bring forth
   Some monstrous malefactor. Prithee, friend,
   Pour out the pack of matter to mine ear,
   The good and bad together: he's friends with Caesar:
   In state of health thou say'st; and thou say'st free.
Messenger
   Free, madam! no; I made no such report:
   He's bound unto Octavia.
CLEOPATRA
   For what good turn?
Messenger
   For the best turn i' the bed.
CLEOPATRA
   I am pale, Charmian.
Messenger
   Madam, he's married to Octavia.
CLEOPATRA
   The most infectious pestilence upon thee!

Strikes him down

Messenger
   Good madam, patience.
CLEOPATRA
   What say you? Hence,

Strikes him again

  Horrible villain! or I'll spurn thine eyes
  Like balls before me; I'll unhair thy head:

She hales him up and down

  Thou shalt be whipp'd with wire, and stew'd in brine,
  Smarting in lingering pickle.

Messenger
  Gracious madam,
  I that do bring the news made not the match.

CLEOPATRA
  Say 'tis not so, a province I will give thee,
  And make thy fortunes proud: the blow thou hadst
  Shall make thy peace for moving me to rage;
  And I will boot thee with what gift beside
  Thy modesty can beg.

Messenger
  He's married, madam.

CLEOPATRA
  Rogue, thou hast lived too long.

Draws a knife

Messenger
  Nay, then I'll run.
  What mean you, madam? I have made no fault.

Exit

CHARMIAN
  Good madam, keep yourself within yourself:
  The man is innocent.

CLEOPATRA
  Some innocents 'scape not the thunderbolt.
  Melt Egypt into Nile! and kindly creatures
  Turn all to serpents! Call the slave again:

The Tragedie of Anthonie and Cleopatra — Act II

Though I am mad, I will not bite him: call.
CHARMIAN
He is afeard to come.
CLEOPATRA
I will not hurt him.

Exit CHARMIAN

These hands do lack nobility, that they strike
A meaner than myself; since I myself
Have given myself the cause.

Re-enter CHARMIAN and Messenger

Come hither, sir.
Though it be honest, it is never good
To bring bad news: give to a gracious message.
An host of tongues; but let ill tidings tell
Themselves when they be felt.
Messenger
I have done my duty.
CLEOPATRA
Is he married?
I cannot hate thee worser than I do,
If thou again say 'Yes.'
Messenger
He's married, madam.
CLEOPATRA
The gods confound thee! dost thou hold there still?
Messenger
Should I lie, madam?
CLEOPATRA
O, I would thou didst,
So half my Egypt were submerged and made
A cistern for scaled snakes! Go, get thee hence:
Hadst thou Narcissus in thy face, to me
Thou wouldst appear most ugly. He is married?

Messenger
  I crave your highness' pardon.
CLEOPATRA
  He is married?
Messenger
  Take no offence that I would not offend you:
  To punish me for what you make me do.
  Seems much unequal: he's married to Octavia.
CLEOPATRA
  O, that his fault should make a knave of thee,
  That art not what thou'rt sure of! Get thee hence:
  The merchandise which thou hast brought from Rome
  Are all too dear for me: lie they upon thy hand,
  And be undone by 'em!

Exit Messenger

CHARMIAN
  Good your highness, patience.
CLEOPATRA
  In praising Antony, I have dispraised Caesar.
CHARMIAN
  Many times, madam.
CLEOPATRA
  I am paid for't now.
  Lead me from hence:
  I faint: O Iras, Charmian! 'tis no matter.
  Go to the fellow, good Alexas; bid him
  Report the feature of Octavia, her years,
  Her inclination, let him not leave out
  The colour of her hair: bring me word quickly.

Exit ALEXAS

  Let him for ever go:--let him not--Charmian,
  Though he be painted one way like a Gorgon,

The Tragedie of Anthonie and Cleopatra — Act II

    The other way's a Mars. Bid you Alexas
        To MARDIAN
    Bring me word how tall she is. Pity me, Charmian,
    But do not speak to me. Lead me to my chamber.

Exeunt

SCENE VI.
Near Misenum.

Flourish. Enter POMPEY and MENAS at one door, with drum and trumpet: at another, OCTAVIUS CAESAR, MARK ANTONY, LEPIDUS, DOMITIUS ENOBARBUS, MECAENAS, with Soldiers marching

POMPEY
    Your hostages I have, so have you mine;
    And we shall talk before we fight.
OCTAVIUS CAESAR
    Most meet
    That first we come to words; and therefore have we
    Our written purposes before us sent;
    Which, if thou hast consider'd, let us know
    If 'twill tie up thy discontented sword,
    And carry back to Sicily much tall youth
    That else must perish here.
POMPEY
    To you all three,
    The senators alone of this great world,
    Chief factors for the gods, I do not know
    Wherefore my father should revengers want,
    Having a son and friends; since Julius Caesar,
    Who at Philippi the good Brutus ghosted,
    There saw you labouring for him. What was't

    That moved pale Cassius to conspire; and what
    Made the all-honour'd, honest Roman, Brutus,
    With the arm'd rest, courtiers and beauteous freedom,
    To drench the Capitol; but that they would
    Have one man but a man? And that is it
    Hath made me rig my navy; at whose burthen
    The anger'd ocean foams; with which I meant
    To scourge the ingratitude that despiteful Rome
    Cast on my noble father.

OCTAVIUS CAESAR
    Take your time.

MARK ANTONY
    Thou canst not fear us, Pompey, with thy sails;
    We'll speak with thee at sea: at land, thou know'st
    How much we do o'er-count thee.

POMPEY
    At land, indeed,
    Thou dost o'er-count me of my father's house:
    But, since the cuckoo builds not for himself,
    Remain in't as thou mayst.

LEPIDUS
    Be pleased to tell us--
    For this is from the present--how you take
    The offers we have sent you.

OCTAVIUS CAESAR
    There's the point.

MARK ANTONY
    Which do not be entreated to, but weigh
    What it is worth embraced.

OCTAVIUS CAESAR
    And what may follow,
    To try a larger fortune.

POMPEY
    You have made me offer

The Tragedie of Anthonie and Cleopatra — Act II

   Of Sicily, Sardinia; and I must
   Rid all the sea of pirates; then, to send
   Measures of wheat to Rome; this 'greed upon
   To part with unhack'd edges, and bear back
   Our targes undinted.

OCTAVIUS CAESAR MARK ANTONY LEPIDUS
   That's our offer.

POMPEY
   Know, then,
   I came before you here a man prepared
   To take this offer: but Mark Antony
   Put me to some impatience: though I lose
   The praise of it by telling, you must know,
   When Caesar and your brother were at blows,
   Your mother came to Sicily and did find
   Her welcome friendly.

MARK ANTONY
   I have heard it, Pompey;
   And am well studied for a liberal thanks
   Which I do owe you.

POMPEY
   Let me have your hand:
   I did not think, sir, to have met you here.

MARK ANTONY
   The beds i' the east are soft; and thanks to you,
   That call'd me timelier than my purpose hither;
   For I have gain'd by 't.

OCTAVIUS CAESAR
   Since I saw you last,
   There is a change upon you.

POMPEY
   Well, I know not
   What counts harsh fortune casts upon my face;
   But in my bosom shall she never come,

To make my heart her vassal.
LEPIDUS
  Well met here.
POMPEY
  I hope so, Lepidus. Thus we are agreed:
  I crave our composition may be written,
  And seal'd between us.
OCTAVIUS CAESAR
  That's the next to do.
POMPEY
  We'll feast each other ere we part; and let's
  Draw lots who shall begin.
MARK ANTONY
  That will I, Pompey.
POMPEY
  No, Antony, take the lot: but, first
  Or last, your fine Egyptian cookery
  Shall have the fame. I have heard that Julius Caesar
  Grew fat with feasting there.
MARK ANTONY
  You have heard much.
POMPEY
  I have fair meanings, sir.
MARK ANTONY
  And fair words to them.
POMPEY
  Then so much have I heard:
  And I have heard, Apollodorus carried--
DOMITIUS ENOBARBUS
  No more of that: he did so.
POMPEY
  What, I pray you?
DOMITIUS ENOBARBUS
  A certain queen to Caesar in a mattress.

The Tragedie of Anthonie and Cleopatra — Act II

POMPEY
  I know thee now: how farest thou, soldier?
DOMITIUS ENOBARBUS
  Well;
  And well am like to do; for, I perceive,
  Four feasts are toward.
POMPEY
  Let me shake thy hand;
  I never hated thee: I have seen thee fight,
  When I have envied thy behavior.
DOMITIUS ENOBARBUS
  Sir,
  I never loved you much; but I ha' praised ye,
  When you have well deserved ten times as much
  As I have said you did.
POMPEY
  Enjoy thy plainness,
  It nothing ill becomes thee.
  Aboard my galley I invite you all:
  Will you lead, lords?
OCTAVIUS CAESAR MARK ANTONY LEPIDUS
  Show us the way, sir.
POMPEY
  Come.

        Exeunt all but MENAS and ENOBARBUS

MENAS
      [Aside]
Thy father, Pompey, would ne'er have
  made this treaty.--You and I have known, sir.
DOMITIUS ENOBARBUS
  At sea, I think.
MENAS
  We have, sir.

DOMITIUS ENOBARBUS
  You have done well by water.
MENAS
  And you by land.
DOMITIUS ENOBARBUS
  I will praise any man that will praise me; though it cannot be denied what I have done by land.
MENAS
  Nor what I have done by water.
DOMITIUS ENOBARBUS
  Yes, something you can deny for your own safety: you have been a great thief by sea.
MENAS
  And you by land.
DOMITIUS ENOBARBUS
  There I deny my land service. But give me your hand, Menas: if our eyes had authority, here they might take two thieves kissing.
MENAS
  All men's faces are true, whatsome'er their hands are.
DOMITIUS ENOBARBUS
  But there is never a fair woman has a true face.
MENAS
  No slander; they steal hearts.
DOMITIUS ENOBARBUS
  We came hither to fight with you.
MENAS
  For my part, I am sorry it is turned to a drinking. Pompey doth this day laugh away his fortune.
DOMITIUS ENOBARBUS
  If he do, sure, he cannot weep't back again.
MENAS
  You've said, sir. We looked not for Mark Antony here: pray you, is he married to Cleopatra?

DOMITIUS ENOBARBUS
   Caesar's sister is called Octavia.
MENAS
   True, sir; she was the wife of Caius Marcellus.
DOMITIUS ENOBARBUS
   But she is now the wife of Marcus Antonius.
MENAS
   Pray ye, sir?
DOMITIUS ENOBARBUS
   'Tis true.
MENAS
   Then is Caesar and he for ever knit together.
DOMITIUS ENOBARBUS
   If I were bound to divine of this unity, I would
   not prophesy so.
MENAS
   I think the policy of that purpose made more in the
   marriage than the love of the parties.
DOMITIUS ENOBARBUS
   I think so too. But you shall find, the band that
   seems to tie their friendship together will be the
   very strangler of their amity: Octavia is of a
   holy, cold, and still conversation.
MENAS
   Who would not have his wife so?
DOMITIUS ENOBARBUS
   Not he that himself is not so; which is Mark Antony.
   He will to his Egyptian dish again: then shall the
   sighs of Octavia blow the fire up in Caesar; and, as
   I said before, that which is the strength of their
   amity shall prove the immediate author of their
   variance. Antony will use his affection where it is:
   he married but his occasion here.

MENAS
   And thus it may be. Come, sir, will you aboard?
   I have a health for you.
DOMITIUS ENOBARBUS
   I shall take it, sir: we have used our throats in Egypt.
MENAS
   Come, let's away.

Exeunt

SCENE VII.
On board POMPEY's galley, off Misenum.

Music plays. Enter two or three Servants with a banquet

First Servant
   Here they'll be, man. Some o' their plants are
   ill-rooted already: the least wind i' the world
   will blow them down.
Second Servant
   Lepidus is high-coloured.
First Servant
   They have made him drink alms-drink.
Second Servant
   As they pinch one another by the disposition, he
   cries out 'No more;' reconciles them to his
   entreaty, and himself to the drink.
First Servant
   But it raises the greater war between him and
   his discretion.
Second Servant
   Why, this is to have a name in great men's
   fellowship: I had as lief have a reed that will do
   me no service as a partisan I could not heave.

The Tragedie of Anthonie and Cleopatra — Act II

First Servant
> To be called into a huge sphere, and not to be seen
> to move in't, are the holes where eyes should be,
> which pitifully disaster the cheeks.

> *A sennet sounded. Enter OCTAVIUS CAESAR, MARK ANTONY, LEPIDUS, POMPEY, AGRIPPA, MECAENAS, DOMITIUS ENOBARBUS, MENAS, with other captains*

MARK ANTONY
> *[To OCTAVIUS CAESAR]*
> Thus do they, sir: they take
> the flow o' the Nile
> By certain scales i' the pyramid; they know,
> By the height, the lowness, or the mean, if dearth
> Or foison follow: the higher Nilus swells,
> The more it promises: as it ebbs, the seedsman
> Upon the slime and ooze scatters his grain,
> And shortly comes to harvest.

LEPIDUS
> You've strange serpents there.

MARK ANTONY
> Ay, Lepidus.

LEPIDUS
> Your serpent of Egypt is bred now of your mud by the
> operation of your sun: so is your crocodile.

MARK ANTONY
> They are so.

POMPEY
> Sit,--and some wine! A health to Lepidus!

LEPIDUS
> I am not so well as I should be, but I'll ne'er out.

DOMITIUS ENOBARBUS
> Not till you have slept; I fear me you'll be in till then.

LEPIDUS
  Nay, certainly, I have heard the Ptolemies'
  pyramises are very goodly things; without
  contradiction, I have heard that.
MENAS
         [Aside to POMPEY]
  Pompey, a word.
POMPEY
         [Aside to MENAS]
  Say in mine ear:
  what is't?
MENAS
         [Aside to POMPEY]
  Forsake thy seat, I do beseech
  thee, captain,
  And hear me speak a word.
POMPEY
         [Aside to MENAS]
  Forbear me till anon.
  This wine for Lepidus!
LEPIDUS
  What manner o' thing is your crocodile?
MARK ANTONY
  It is shaped, sir, like itself; and it is as broad
  as it hath breadth: it is just so high as it is,
  and moves with its own organs: it lives by that
  which nourisheth it; and the elements once out of
  it, it transmigrates.
LEPIDUS
  What colour is it of?
MARK ANTONY
  Of it own colour too.
LEPIDUS
  'Tis a strange serpent.

The Tragedie of Anthonie and Cleopatra – Act II

MARK ANTONY
  'Tis so. And the tears of it are wet.
OCTAVIUS CAESAR
  Will this description satisfy him?
MARK ANTONY
  With the health that Pompey gives him, else he is a very epicure.
POMPEY
  [Aside to MENAS]
  Go hang, sir, hang! Tell me of
  that? away!
  Do as I bid you. Where's this cup I call'd for?
MENAS
  [Aside to POMPEY]
  If for the sake of merit thou
  wilt hear me,
  Rise from thy stool.
POMPEY
  [Aside to MENAS]
  I think thou'rt mad.
  The matter?

  Rises, and walks aside

MENAS
  I have ever held my cap off to thy fortunes.
POMPEY
  Thou hast served me with much faith. What's else to say?
  Be jolly, lords.
MARK ANTONY
  These quick-sands, Lepidus,
  Keep off them, for you sink.
MENAS
  Wilt thou be lord of all the world?

POMPEY
  What say'st thou?
MENAS
  Wilt thou be lord of the whole world? That's twice.
POMPEY
  How should that be?
MENAS
  But entertain it,
  And, though thou think me poor, I am the man
  Will give thee all the world.
POMPEY
  Hast thou drunk well?
MENAS
  Now, Pompey, I have kept me from the cup.
  Thou art, if thou darest be, the earthly Jove:
  Whate'er the ocean pales, or sky inclips,
  Is thine, if thou wilt ha't.
POMPEY
  Show me which way.
MENAS
  These three world-sharers, these competitors,
  Are in thy vessel: let me cut the cable;
  And, when we are put off, fall to their throats:
  All there is thine.
POMPEY
  Ah, this thou shouldst have done,
  And not have spoke on't! In me 'tis villany;
  In thee't had been good service. Thou must know,
  'Tis not my profit that does lead mine honour;
  Mine honour, it. Repent that e'er thy tongue
  Hath so betray'd thine act: being done unknown,
  I should have found it afterwards well done;
  But must condemn it now. Desist, and drink.

MENAS
> *[Aside]*
> For this,
> I'll never follow thy pall'd fortunes more.
> Who seeks, and will not take when once 'tis offer'd,
> Shall never find it more.

POMPEY
> This health to Lepidus!

MARK ANTONY
> Bear him ashore. I'll pledge it for him, Pompey.

DOMITIUS ENOBARBUS
> Here's to thee, Menas!

MENAS
> Enobarbus, welcome!

POMPEY
> Fill till the cup be hid.

DOMITIUS ENOBARBUS
> There's a strong fellow, Menas.

Pointing to the Attendant who carries off LEPIDUS

MENAS
> Why?

DOMITIUS ENOBARBUS
> A' bears the third part of the world, man; see'st not?

MENAS
> The third part, then, is drunk: would it were all,
> That it might go on wheels!

DOMITIUS ENOBARBUS
> Drink thou; increase the reels.

MENAS
> Come.

POMPEY
> This is not yet an Alexandrian feast.

MARK ANTONY
   It ripens towards it. Strike the vessels, ho?
   Here is to Caesar!
OCTAVIUS CAESAR
   I could well forbear't.
   It's monstrous labour, when I wash my brain,
   And it grows fouler.
MARK ANTONY
   Be a child o' the time.
OCTAVIUS CAESAR
   Possess it, I'll make answer:
   But I had rather fast from all four days
   Than drink so much in one.
DOMITIUS ENOBARBUS
   Ha, my brave emperor!
         To MARK ANTONY
   Shall we dance now the Egyptian Bacchanals,
   And celebrate our drink?
POMPEY
   Let's ha't, good soldier.
MARK ANTONY
   Come, let's all take hands,
   Till that the conquering wine hath steep'd our sense
   In soft and delicate Lethe.
DOMITIUS ENOBARBUS
   All take hands.
   Make battery to our ears with the loud music:
   The while I'll place you: then the boy shall sing;
   The holding every man shall bear as loud
   As his strong sides can volley.

   Music plays. DOMITIUS ENOBARBUS places them hand in hand
            THE SONG.
   Come, thou monarch of the vine,

The Tragedie of Anthonie and Cleopatra — Act II

    Plumpy Bacchus with pink eyne!
    In thy fats our cares be drown'd,
    With thy grapes our hairs be crown'd:
    Cup us, till the world go round,
    Cup us, till the world go round!

OCTAVIUS CAESAR
    What would you more? Pompey, good night. Good brother,
    Let me request you off: our graver business
    Frowns at this levity. Gentle lords, let's part;
    You see we have burnt our cheeks: strong Enobarb
    Is weaker than the wine; and mine own tongue
    Splits what it speaks: the wild disguise hath almost
    Antick'd us all. What needs more words? Good night.
    Good Antony, your hand.

POMPEY
    I'll try you on the shore.

MARK ANTONY
    And shall, sir; give's your hand.

POMPEY
    O Antony,
    You have my father's house,--But, what? we are friends.
    Come, down into the boat.

DOMITIUS ENOBARBUS
    Take heed you fall not.

    Exeunt all but DOMITIUS ENOBARBUS and MENAS
    Menas, I'll not on shore.

MENAS
    No, to my cabin.
    These drums! these trumpets, flutes! what!
    Let Neptune hear we bid a loud farewell
    To these great fellows: sound and be hang'd, sound out!

        Sound a flourish, with drums

The Tragedie of Anthonie and Cleopatra — Act II

DOMITIUS ENOBARBUS
  Ho! says a' There's my cap.
MENAS
  Ho! Noble captain, come.

Exeunt

ACT III

SCENE I.
A plain in Syria.

Enter VENTIDIUS as it were in triumph, with SILIUS, and other Romans, Officers, and Soldiers; the dead body of PACORUS borne before him

VENTIDIUS
　Now, darting Parthia, art thou struck; and now
　Pleased fortune does of Marcus Crassus' death
　Make me revenger. Bear the king's son's body
　Before our army. Thy Pacorus, Orodes,
　Pays this for Marcus Crassus.
SILIUS
　Noble Ventidius,
　Whilst yet with Parthian blood thy sword is warm,
　The fugitive Parthians follow; spur through Media,
　Mesopotamia, and the shelters whither
　The routed fly: so thy grand captain Antony
　Shall set thee on triumphant chariots and
　Put garlands on thy head.
VENTIDIUS
　O Silius, Silius,
　I have done enough; a lower place, note well,
　May make too great an act: for learn this, Silius;
　Better to leave undone, than by our deed
　Acquire too high a fame when him we serve's away.
　Caesar and Antony have ever won
　More in their officer than person: Sossius,
　One of my place in Syria, his lieutenant,
　For quick accumulation of renown,

Which he achieved by the minute, lost his favour.
Who does i' the wars more than his captain can
Becomes his captain's captain: and ambition,
The soldier's virtue, rather makes choice of loss,
Than gain which darkens him.
I could do more to do Antonius good,
But 'twould offend him; and in his offence
Should my performance perish.

SILIUS
Thou hast, Ventidius,
that
Without the which a soldier, and his sword,
Grants scarce distinction. Thou wilt write to Antony!

VENTIDIUS
I'll humbly signify what in his name,
That magical word of war, we have effected;
How, with his banners and his well-paid ranks,
The ne'er-yet-beaten horse of Parthia
We have jaded out o' the field.

SILIUS
Where is he now?

VENTIDIUS
He purposeth to Athens: whither, with what haste
The weight we must convey with's will permit,
We shall appear before him. On there; pass along!

Exeunt

The Tragedie of Anthonie and Cleopatra — Act III

SCENE II.

Rome. An ante-chamber in OCTAVIUS CAESAR's house.

Enter AGRIPPA at one door, DOMITIUS ENOBARBUS at another

AGRIPPA
 What, are the brothers parted?
DOMITIUS ENOBARBUS
 They have dispatch'd with Pompey, he is gone;
 The other three are sealing. Octavia weeps
 To part from Rome; Caesar is sad; and Lepidus,
 Since Pompey's feast, as Menas says, is troubled
 With the green sickness.
AGRIPPA
 'Tis a noble Lepidus.
DOMITIUS ENOBARBUS
 A very fine one: O, how he loves Caesar!
AGRIPPA
 Nay, but how dearly he adores Mark Antony!
DOMITIUS ENOBARBUS
 Caesar? Why, he's the Jupiter of men.
AGRIPPA
 What's Antony? The god of Jupiter.
DOMITIUS ENOBARBUS
 Spake you of Caesar? How! the non-pareil!
AGRIPPA
 O Antony! O thou Arabian bird!
DOMITIUS ENOBARBUS
 Would you praise Caesar, say 'Caesar:' go no further.
AGRIPPA
 Indeed, he plied them both with excellent praises.
DOMITIUS ENOBARBUS
 But he loves Caesar best; yet he loves Antony:

The Tragedie of Anthonie and Cleopatra — Act III

Ho! hearts, tongues, figures, scribes, bards, poets, cannot
Think, speak, cast, write, sing, number, ho!
His love to Antony. But as for Caesar,
Kneel down, kneel down, and wonder.

AGRIPPA
Both he loves.

DOMITIUS ENOBARBUS
They are his shards, and he their beetle.

Trumpets within

So;
This is to horse. Adieu, noble Agrippa.

AGRIPPA
Good fortune, worthy soldier; and farewell.

Enter OCTAVIUS CAESAR, MARK ANTONY, LEPIDUS, and OCTAVIA

MARK ANTONY
No further, sir.

OCTAVIUS CAESAR
You take from me a great part of myself;
Use me well in 't. Sister, prove such a wife
As my thoughts make thee, and as my farthest band
Shall pass on thy approof. Most noble Antony,
Let not the piece of virtue, which is set
Betwixt us as the cement of our love,
To keep it builded, be the ram to batter
The fortress of it; for better might we
Have loved without this mean, if on both parts
This be not cherish'd.

MARK ANTONY
Make me not offended
In your distrust.

The Tragedie of Anthonie and Cleopatra — Act III

OCTAVIUS CAESAR
  I have said.
MARK ANTONY
  You shall not find,
  Though you be therein curious, the least cause
  For what you seem to fear: so, the gods keep you,
  And make the hearts of Romans serve your ends!
  We will here part.
OCTAVIUS CAESAR
  Farewell, my dearest sister, fare thee well:
  The elements be kind to thee, and make
  Thy spirits all of comfort! fare thee well.
OCTAVIA
  My noble brother!
MARK ANTONY
  The April 's in her eyes: it is love's spring,
  And these the showers to bring it on. Be cheerful.
OCTAVIA
  Sir, look well to my husband's house; and--
OCTAVIUS CAESAR
  What, Octavia?
OCTAVIA
  I'll tell you in your ear.
MARK ANTONY
  Her tongue will not obey her heart, nor can
  Her heart inform her tongue,--the swan's
  down-feather,
  That stands upon the swell at full of tide,
  And neither way inclines.
DOMITIUS ENOBARBUS
       [Aside to AGRIPPA]
  Will Caesar weep?

The Tragedie of Anthonie and Cleopatra — Act III

AGRIPPA
> *[Aside to DOMITIUS ENOBARBUS]*
> He has a cloud in 's face.

DOMITIUS ENOBARBUS
> *[Aside to AGRIPPA]*
> He were the worse for that,
> were he a horse;
> So is he, being a man.

AGRIPPA
> *[Aside to DOMITIUS ENOBARBUS]*
> Why, Enobarbus,
> When Antony found Julius Caesar dead,
> He cried almost to roaring; and he wept
> When at Philippi he found Brutus slain.

DOMITIUS ENOBARBUS
> *[Aside to AGRIPPA]*
> That year, indeed, he was
> troubled with a rheum;
> What willingly he did confound he wail'd,
> Believe't, till I wept too.

OCTAVIUS CAESAR
> No, sweet Octavia,
> You shall hear from me still; the time shall not
> Out-go my thinking on you.

MARK ANTONY
> Come, sir, come;
> I'll wrestle with you in my strength of love:
> Look, here I have you; thus I let you go,
> And give you to the gods.

OCTAVIUS CAESAR
> Adieu; be happy!

LEPIDUS
> Let all the number of the stars give light
> To thy fair way!

OCTAVIUS CAESAR
Farewell, fa rewell!

Kisses OCTAVIA

MARK ANTONY
Farewell!

Trumpets sound. Exeunt

SCENE III.
Alexandria. CLEOPATRA's palace.

Enter CLEOPATRA, CHARMIAN, IRAS, and ALEXAS

CLEOPATRA
Where is the fellow?
ALEXAS
Half afeard to come.
CLEOPATRA
Go to, go to.

Enter the Messenger as before

Come hither, sir.
ALEXAS
Good majesty,
Herod of Jewry dare not look upon you
But when you are well pleased.
CLEOPATRA
That Herod's head
I'll have: but how, when Antony is gone
Through whom I might command it? Come thou near.
Messenger
Most gracious majesty,--

CLEOPATRA
  Didst thou behold Octavia?
Messenger
  Ay, dread queen.
CLEOPATRA
  Where?
Messenger
  Madam, in Rome;
  I look'd her in the face, and saw her led
  Between her brother and Mark Antony.
CLEOPATRA
  Is she as tall as me?
Messenger
  She is not, madam.
CLEOPATRA
  Didst hear her speak? is she shrill-tongued or low?
Messenger
  Madam, I heard her speak; she is low-voiced.
CLEOPATRA
  That's not so good: he cannot like her long.
CHARMIAN
  Like her! O Isis! 'tis impossible.
CLEOPATRA
  I think so, Charmian: dull of tongue, and dwarfish!
  What majesty is in her gait? Remember,
  If e'er thou look'dst on majesty.
Messenger
  She creeps:
  Her motion and her station are as one;
  She shows a body rather than a life,
  A statue than a breather.
CLEOPATRA
  Is this certain?

Messenger
 Or I have no observance.
CHARMIAN
 Three in Egypt
 Cannot make better note.
CLEOPATRA
 He's very knowing;
 I do perceive't: there's nothing in her yet:
 The fellow has good judgment.
CHARMIAN
 Excellent.
CLEOPATRA
 Guess at her years, I prithee.
Messenger
 Madam,
 She was a widow,--
CLEOPATRA
 Widow! Charmian, hark.
Messenger
 And I do think she's thirty.
CLEOPATRA
 Bear'st thou her face in mind? is't long or round?
Messenger
 Round even to faultiness.
CLEOPATRA
 For the most part, too, they are foolish that are so.
 Her hair, what colour?
Messenger
 Brown, madam: and her forehead
 As low as she would wish it.
CLEOPATRA
 There's gold for thee.
 Thou must not take my former sharpness ill:
 I will employ thee back again; I find thee

Most fit for business: go make thee ready;
Our letters are prepared.

Exit Messenger

CHARMIAN
  A proper man.
CLEOPATRA
  Indeed, he is so: I repent me much
  That so I harried him. Why, methinks, by him,
  This creature's no such thing.
CHARMIAN
  Nothing, madam.
CLEOPATRA
  The man hath seen some majesty, and should know.
CHARMIAN
  Hath he seen majesty? Isis else defend,
  And serving you so long!
CLEOPATRA
  I have one thing more to ask him yet, good Charmian:
  But 'tis no matter; thou shalt bring him to me
  Where I will write. All may be well enough.
CHARMIAN
  I warrant you, madam.

Exeunt

The Tragedie of Anthonie and Cleopatra — Act III

SCENE IV.
Athens. A room in MARK ANTONY's house.

Enter MARK ANTONY and OCTAVIA

MARK ANTONY
   Nay, nay, Octavia, not only that,--
   That were excusable, that, and thousands more
   Of semblable import,--but he hath waged
   New wars 'gainst Pompey; made his will, and read it
   To public ear:
   Spoke scantly of me: when perforce he could not
   But pay me terms of honour, cold and sickly
   He vented them; most narrow measure lent me:
   When the best hint was given him, he not took't,
   Or did it from his teeth.
OCTAVIA
   O my good lord,
   Believe not all; or, if you must believe,
   Stomach not all. A more unhappy lady,
   If this division chance, ne'er stood between,
   Praying for both parts:
   The good gods me presently,
   When I shall pray, 'O bless my lord and husband!'
   Undo that prayer, by crying out as loud,
   'O, bless my brother!' Husband win, win brother,
   Prays, and destroys the prayer; no midway
   'Twixt these extremes at all.
MARK ANTONY
   Gentle Octavia,
   Let your best love draw to that point, which seeks
   Best to preserve it: if I lose mine honour,
   I lose myself: better I were not yours
   Than yours so branchless. But, as you requested,

Yourself shall go between 's: the mean time, lady,
　　I'll raise the preparation of a war
　　Shall stain your brother: make your soonest haste;
　　So your desires are yours.
OCTAVIA
　　Thanks to my lord.
　　The Jove of power make me most weak, most weak,
　　Your reconciler! Wars 'twixt you twain would be
　　As if the world should cleave, and that slain men
　　Should solder up the rift.
MARK ANTONY
　　When it appears to you where this begins,
　　Turn your displeasure that way: for our faults
　　Can never be so equal, that your love
　　Can equally move with them. Provide your going;
　　Choose your own company, and command what cost
　　Your heart has mind to.

Exeunt

SCENE V.
The same. Another room.

Enter DOMITIUS ENOBARBUS and EROS, meeting

DOMITIUS ENOBARBUS
　　How now, friend Eros!
EROS
　　There's strange news come, sir.
DOMITIUS ENOBARBUS
　　What, man?
EROS
　　Caesar and Lepidus have made wars upon Pompey.

DOMITIUS ENOBARBUS
This is old: what is the success?
EROS
Caesar, having made use of him in the wars 'gainst
Pompey, presently denied him rivality; would not let
him partake in the glory of the action: and not
resting here, accuses him of letters he had formerly
wrote to Pompey; upon his own appeal, seizes him: so
the poor third is up, till death enlarge his confine.
DOMITIUS ENOBARBUS
Then, world, thou hast a pair of chaps, no more;
And throw between them all the food thou hast,
They'll grind the one the other. Where's Antony?
EROS
He's walking in the garden--thus; and spurns
The rush that lies before him; cries, 'Fool Lepidus!'
And threats the throat of that his officer
That murder'd Pompey.
DOMITIUS ENOBARBUS
Our great navy's rigg'd.
EROS
For Italy and Caesar. More, Domitius;
My lord desires you presently: my news
I might have told hereafter.
DOMITIUS ENOBARBUS
'Twill be naught:
But let it be. Bring me to Antony.
EROS
Come, sir.

Exeunt

SCENE VI.
Rome. OCTAVIUS CAESAR's house.

Enter OCTAVIUS CAESAR, AGRIPPA, and MECAENAS

OCTAVIUS CAESAR
   Contemning Rome, he has done all this, and more,
   In Alexandria: here's the manner of 't:
   I' the market-place, on a tribunal silver'd,
   Cleopatra and himself in chairs of gold
   Were publicly enthroned: at the feet sat
   Caesarion, whom they call my father's son,
   And all the unlawful issue that their lust
   Since then hath made between them. Unto her
   He gave the stablishment of Egypt; made her
   Of lower Syria, Cyprus, Lydia,
   Absolute queen.
MECAENAS
   This in the public eye?
OCTAVIUS CAESAR
   I' the common show-place, where they exercise.
   His sons he there proclaim'd the kings of kings:
   Great Media, Parthia, and Armenia.
   He gave to Alexander; to Ptolemy he assign'd
   Syria, Cilicia, and Phoenicia: she
   In the habiliments of the goddess Isis
   That day appear'd; and oft before gave audience,
   As 'tis reported, so.
MECAENAS
   Let Rome be thus Inform'd.
AGRIPPA
   Who, queasy with his insolence
   Already, will their good thoughts call from him.

OCTAVIUS CAESAR
  The people know it; and have now received
  His accusations.
AGRIPPA
  Who does he accuse?
OCTAVIUS CAESAR
  Caesar: and that, having in Sicily
  Sextus Pompeius spoil'd, we had not rated him
  His part o' the isle: then does he say, he lent me
  Some shipping unrestored: lastly, he frets
  That Lepidus of the triumvirate
  Should be deposed; and, being, that we detain
  All his revenue.
AGRIPPA
  Sir, this should be answer'd.
OCTAVIUS CAESAR
  'Tis done already, and the messenger gone.
  I have told him, Lepidus was grown too cruel;
  That he his high authority abused,
  And did deserve his change: for what I have conquer'd,
  I grant him part; but then, in his Armenia,
  And other of his conquer'd kingdoms, I
  Demand the like.
MECAENAS
  He'll never yield to that.
OCTAVIUS CAESAR
  Nor must not then be yielded to in this.

Enter OCTAVIA with her train

OCTAVIA
  Hail, Caesar, and my lord! hail, most dear Caesar!
OCTAVIUS CAESAR
  That ever I should call thee castaway!

OCTAVIA
  You have not call'd me so, nor have you cause.
OCTAVIUS CAESAR
    Why have you stol'n upon us thus! You come not
    Like Caesar's sister: the wife of Antony
    Should have an army for an usher, and
    The neighs of horse to tell of her approach
    Long ere she did appear; the trees by the way
    Should have borne men; and expectation fainted,
    Longing for what it had not; nay, the dust
    Should have ascended to the roof of heaven,
    Raised by your populous troops: but you are come
    A market-maid to Rome; and have prevented
    The ostentation of our love, which, left unshown,
    Is often left unloved; we should have met you
    By sea and land; supplying every stage
    With an augmented greeting.
OCTAVIA
    Good my lord,
    To come thus was I not constrain'd, but did
    On my free will. My lord, Mark Antony,
    Hearing that you prepared for war, acquainted
    My grieved ear withal; whereon, I begg'd
    His pardon for return.
OCTAVIUS CAESAR

    Which soon he granted,
    Being an obstruct 'tween his lust and him.
OCTAVIA
    Do not say so, my lord.
OCTAVIUS CAESAR
    I have eyes upon him,
    And his affairs come to me on the wind.
    Where is he now?

The Tragedie of Anthonie and Cleopatra — Act III

OCTAVIA
  My lord, in Athens.
OCTAVIUS CAESAR
  No, my most wronged sister; Cleopatra
  Hath nodded him to her. He hath given his empire
  Up to a whore; who now are levying
  The kings o' the earth for war; he hath assembled
  Bocchus, the king of Libya; Archelaus,
  Of Cappadocia; Philadelphos, king
  Of Paphlagonia; the Thracian king, Adallas;
  King Malchus of Arabia; King of Pont;
  Herod of Jewry; Mithridates, king
  Of Comagene; Polemon and Amyntas,
  The kings of Mede and Lycaonia,
  With a more larger list of sceptres.
OCTAVIA
  Ay me, most wretched,
  That have my heart parted betwixt two friends
  That do afflict each other!
OCTAVIUS CAESAR
  Welcome hither:
  Your letters did withhold our breaking forth;
  Till we perceived, both how you were wrong led,
  And we in negligent danger. Cheer your heart;
  Be you not troubled with the time, which drives
  O'er your content these strong necessities;
  But let determined things to destiny
  Hold unbewail'd their way. Welcome to Rome;
  Nothing more dear to me. You are abused
  Beyond the mark of thought: and the high gods,
  To do you justice, make them ministers
  Of us and those that love you. Best of comfort;
  And ever welcome to us.

AGRIPPA
  Welcome, lady.
MECAENAS
  Welcome, dear madam.
  Each heart in Rome does love and pity you:
  Only the adulterous Antony, most large
  In his abominations, turns you off;
  And gives his potent regiment to a trull,
  That noises it against us.
OCTAVIA
  Is it so, sir?
OCTAVIUS CAESAR
  Most certain. Sister, welcome: pray you,
  Be ever known to patience: my dear'st sister!

Exeunt

SCENE VII.
Near Actium. MARK ANTONY's camp.

Enter CLEOPATRA and DOMITIUS ENOBARBUS

CLEOPATRA
  I will be even with thee, doubt it not.
DOMITIUS ENOBARBUS
  But why, why, why?
CLEOPATRA
  Thou hast forspoke my being in these wars,
  And say'st it is not fit.
DOMITIUS ENOBARBUS
  Well, is it, is it?
CLEOPATRA
  If not denounced against us, why should not we
  Be there in person?

DOMITIUS ENOBARBUS
[Aside]
  Well, I could reply:
  If we should serve with horse and mares together,
  The horse were merely lost; the mares would bear
  A soldier and his horse.
CLEOPATRA
  What is't you say?
DOMITIUS ENOBARBUS
  Your presence needs must puzzle Antony;
  Take from his heart, take from his brain,
  from's time,
  What should not then be spared. He is already
  Traduced for levity; and 'tis said in Rome
  That Photinus an eunuch and your maids
  Manage this war.
CLEOPATRA
  Sink Rome, and their tongues rot
  That speak against us! A charge we bear i' the war,
  And, as the president of my kingdom, will
  Appear there for a man. Speak not against it:
  I will not stay behind.
DOMITIUS ENOBARBUS
  Nay, I have done.
  Here comes the emperor.

Enter MARK ANTONY and CANIDIUS

MARK ANTONY
  Is it not strange, Canidius,
  That from Tarentum and Brundusium
  He could so quickly cut the Ionian sea,
  And take in Toryne? You have heard on't, sweet?

CLEOPATRA
  Celerity is never more admired
  Than by the negligent.
MARK ANTONY
  A good rebuke,
  Which might have well becomed the best of men,
  To taunt at slackness. Canidius, we
  Will fight with him by sea.
CLEOPATRA
  By sea! what else?
CANIDIUS
  Why will my lord do so?
MARK ANTONY
  For that he dares us to't.
DOMITIUS ENOBARBUS
  So hath my lord dared him to single fight.
CANIDIUS
  Ay, and to wage this battle at Pharsalia.
  Where Caesar fought with Pompey: but these offers,
  Which serve not for his vantage, be shakes off;
  And so should you.
DOMITIUS ENOBARBUS
  Your ships are not well mann'd;
  Your mariners are muleters, reapers, people
  Ingross'd by swift impress; in Caesar's fleet
  Are those that often have 'gainst Pompey fought:
  Their ships are yare; yours, heavy: no disgrace
  Shall fall you for refusing him at sea,
  Being prepared for land.
MARK ANTONY
  By sea, by sea.
DOMITIUS ENOBARBUS
  Most worthy sir, you therein throw away
  The absolute soldiership you have by land;

The Tragedie of Anthonie and Cleopatra — Act III

   Distract your army, which doth most consist
   Of war-mark'd footmen; leave unexecuted
   Your own renowned knowledge; quite forego
   The way which promises assurance; and
   Give up yourself merely to chance and hazard,
   From firm security.
MARK ANTONY
   I'll fight at sea.
CLEOPATRA
   I have sixty sails, Caesar none better.
MARK ANTONY
   Our overplus of shipping will we burn;
   And, with the rest full-mann'd, from the head of Actium
   Beat the approaching Caesar. But if we fail,
   We then can do't at land.

              Enter a Messenger

   Thy business?
Messenger
   The news is true, my lord; he is descried;
   Caesar has taken Toryne.
MARK ANTONY
   Can he be there in person? 'tis impossible;
   Strange that power should be. Canidius,
   Our nineteen legions thou shalt hold by land,
   And our twelve thousand horse. We'll to our ship:
   Away, my Thetis!

              Enter a Soldier

   How now, worthy soldier?
Soldier
   O noble emperor, do not fight by sea;
   Trust not to rotten planks: do you misdoubt
   This sword and these my wounds? Let the Egyptians
   And the Phoenicians go a-ducking; we

Have used to conquer, standing on the earth,
And fighting foot to foot.
MARK ANTONY
Well, well: away!

Exeunt MARK ANTONY, QUEEN CLEOPATRA, and DOMITIUS ENOBARBUS

Soldier
By Hercules, I think I am i' the right.
CANIDIUS
Soldier, thou art: but his whole action grows
Not in the power on't: so our leader's led,
And we are women's men.
Soldier
You keep by land
The legions and the horse whole, do you not?
CANIDIUS
Marcus Octavius, Marcus Justeius,
Publicola, and Caelius, are for sea:
But we keep whole by land. This speed of Caesar's
Carries beyond belief.
Soldier
While he was yet in Rome,
His power went out in such distractions as
Beguiled all spies.
CANIDIUS
Who's his lieutenant, hear you?
Soldier
They say, one Taurus.
CANIDIUS
Well I know the man.

Enter a Messenger

The Tragedie of Anthonie and Cleopatra — Act III

Messenger
　The emperor calls Canidius.
CANIDIUS
　With news the time's with labour, and throes forth,
　Each minute, some.

Exeunt

SCENE VIII.
A plain near Actium.

Enter OCTAVIUS CAESAR, and TAURUS, with his army, marching

OCTAVIUS CAESAR
　Taurus!
TAURUS
　My lord?
OCTAVIUS CAESAR
　Strike not by land; keep whole: provoke not battle,
　Till we have done at sea. Do not exceed
　The prescript of this scroll: our fortune lies
　Upon this jump.

Exeunt

SCENE IX.
Another part of the plain.

Enter MARK ANTONY and DOMITIUS ENOBARBUS

MARK ANTONY
　Set we our squadrons on yond side o' the hill,
　In eye of Caesar's battle; from which place

We may the number of the ships behold,
And so proceed accordingly.

Exeunt

SCENE X.
Another part of the plain.

CANIDIUS marcheth with his land army one way over the stage; and TAURUS, the lieutenant of OCTAVIUS CAESAR, the other way. After their going in, is heard the noise of a sea-fight

Alarum. Enter DOMITIUS ENOBARBUS

DOMITIUS ENOBARBUS
   Naught, naught all, naught! I can behold no longer:
   The Antoniad, the Egyptian admiral,
   With all their sixty, fly and turn the rudder:
   To see't mine eyes are blasted.

Enter SCARUS

SCARUS
   Gods and goddesses,
   All the whole synod of them!
DOMITIUS ENOBARBUS
   What's thy passion!
SCARUS
   The greater cantle of the world is lost
   With very ignorance; we have kiss'd away
   Kingdoms and provinces.
DOMITIUS ENOBARBUS
   How appears the fight?

The Tragedie of Anthonie and Cleopatra — Act III

SCARUS
  On our side like the token'd pestilence,
  Where death is sure. Yon ribaudred nag of Egypt,--
  Whom leprosy o'ertake!--i' the midst o' the fight,
  When vantage like a pair of twins appear'd,
  Both as the same, or rather ours the elder,
  The breese upon her, like a cow in June,
  Hoists sails and flies.
DOMITIUS ENOBARBUS
  That I beheld:
  Mine eyes did sicken at the sight, and could not
  Endure a further view.
SCARUS
  She once being loof'd,
  The noble ruin of her magic, Antony,
  Claps on his sea-wing, and, like a doting mallard,
  Leaving the fight in height, flies after her:
  I never saw an action of such shame;
  Experience, manhood, honour, ne'er before
  Did violate so itself.
DOMITIUS ENOBARBUS
  Alack, alack!

Enter CANIDIUS

CANIDIUS
  Our fortune on the sea is out of breath,
  And sinks most lamentably. Had our general
  Been what he knew himself, it had gone well:
  O, he has given example for our flight,
  Most grossly, by his own!
DOMITIUS ENOBARBUS
  Ay, are you thereabouts?
  Why, then, good night indeed.

CANIDIUS
  Toward Peloponnesus are they fled.
SCARUS
  'Tis easy to't; and there I will attend
  What further comes.
CANIDIUS
  To Caesar will I render
  My legions and my horse: six kings already
  Show me the way of yielding.
DOMITIUS ENOBARBUS
  I'll yet follow
  The wounded chance of Antony, though my reason
  Sits in the wind against me.

Exeunt

SCENE XI.
Alexandria. CLEOPATRA's palace.

Enter MARK ANTONY with Attendants

MARK ANTONY
  Hark! the land bids me tread no more upon't;
  It is ashamed to bear me! Friends, come hither:
  I am so lated in the world, that I
  Have lost my way for ever: I have a ship
  Laden with gold; take that, divide it; fly,
  And make your peace with Caesar.
All
  Fly! not we.
MARK ANTONY
  I have fled myself; and have instructed cowards
  To run and show their shoulders. Friends, be gone;
  I have myself resolved upon a course

The Tragedie of Anthonie and Cleopatra — Act III

Which has no need of you; be gone:
My treasure's in the harbour, take it. O,
I follow'd that I blush to look upon:
My very hairs do mutiny; for the white
Reprove the brown for rashness, and they them
For fear and doting. Friends, be gone: you shall
Have letters from me to some friends that will
Sweep your way for you. Pray you, look not sad,
Nor make replies of loathness: take the hint
Which my despair proclaims; let that be left
Which leaves itself: to the sea-side straightway:
I will possess you of that ship and treasure.
Leave me, I pray, a little: pray you now:
Nay, do so; for, indeed, I have lost command,
Therefore I pray you: I'll see you by and by.

Sits down

Enter CLEOPATRA led by CHARMIAN and IRAS; EROS following

EROS
   Nay, gentle madam, to him, comfort him.
IRAS
   Do, most dear queen.
CHARMIAN
   Do! why: what else?
CLEOPATRA
   Let me sit down. O Juno!
MARK ANTONY
   No, no, no, no, no.
EROS
   See you here, sir?

MARK ANTONY
  O fie, fie, fie!
CHARMIAN
  Madam!
IRAS
  Madam, O good empress!
EROS
  Sir, sir,--
MARK ANTONY
  Yes, my lord, yes; he at Philippi kept
  His sword e'en like a dancer; while I struck
  The lean and wrinkled Cassius; and 'twas I
  That the mad Brutus ended: he alone
  Dealt on lieutenantry, and no practise had
  In the brave squares of war: yet now--No matter.
CLEOPATRA
  Ah, stand by.
EROS
  The queen, my lord, the queen.
IRAS
  Go to him, madam, speak to him:
  He is unqualitied with very shame.
CLEOPATRA
  Well then, sustain him: O!
EROS
  Most noble sir, arise; the queen approaches:
  Her head's declined, and death will seize her, but
  Your comfort makes the rescue.
MARK ANTONY
  I have offended reputation,
  A most unnoble swerving.
EROS
  Sir, the queen.

MARK ANTONY
  O, whither hast thou led me, Egypt? See,
  How I convey my shame out of thine eyes
  By looking back what I have left behind
  'Stroy'd in dishonour.

CLEOPATRA
  O my lord, my lord,
  Forgive my fearful sails! I little thought
  You would have follow'd.

MARK ANTONY
  Egypt, thou knew'st too well
  My heart was to thy rudder tied by the strings,
  And thou shouldst tow me after: o'er my spirit
  Thy full supremacy thou knew'st, and that
  Thy beck might from the bidding of the gods
  Command me.

CLEOPATRA
  O, my pardon!

MARK ANTONY
  Now I must
  To the young man send humble treaties, dodge
  And palter in the shifts of lowness; who
  With half the bulk o' the world play'd as I pleased,
  Making and marring fortunes. You did know
  How much you were my conqueror; and that
  My sword, made weak by my affection, would
  Obey it on all cause.

CLEOPATRA
  Pardon, pardon!

MARK ANTONY
  Fall not a tear, I say; one of them rates
  All that is won and lost: give me a kiss;
  Even this repays me. We sent our schoolmaster;
  Is he come back? Love, I am full of lead.

Some wine, within there, and our viands! Fortune knows
We scorn her most when most she offers blows.

Exeunt

SCENE XII.
Egypt. OCTAVIUS CAESAR's camp.

Enter OCTAVIUS CAESAR, DOLABELLA, THYREUS, with others

OCTAVIUS CAESAR
  Let him appear that's come from Antony.
  Know you him?
DOLABELLA
  Caesar, 'tis his schoolmaster:
  An argument that he is pluck'd, when hither
  He sends so poor a pinion off his wing,
  Which had superfluous kings for messengers
  Not many moons gone by.

Enter EUPHRONIUS, ambassador from MARK ANTONY

OCTAVIUS CAESAR
  Approach, and speak.
EUPHRONIUS
  Such as I am, I come from Antony:
  I was of late as petty to his ends
  As is the morn-dew on the myrtle-leaf
  To his grand sea.
OCTAVIUS CAESAR
  Be't so: declare thine office.
EUPHRONIUS
  Lord of his fortunes he salutes thee, and
  Requires to live in Egypt: which not granted,

The Tragedie of Anthonie and Cleopatra — Act III

He lessens his requests; and to thee sues
To let him breathe between the heavens and earth,
A private man in Athens: this for him.
Next, Cleopatra does confess thy greatness;
Submits her to thy might; and of thee craves
The circle of the Ptolemies for her heirs,
Now hazarded to thy grace.

OCTAVIUS CAESAR

For Antony,
I have no ears to his request. The queen
Of audience nor desire shall fail, so she
From Egypt drive her all-disgraced friend,
Or take his life there: this if she perform,
She shall not sue unheard. So to them both.

EUPHRONIUS

Fortune pursue thee!

OCTAVIUS CAESAR

Bring him through the bands.

Exit EUPHRONIUS

To THYREUS

From Antony win Cleopatra: promise,
And in our name, what she requires; add more,
From thine invention, offers: women are not
In their best fortunes strong; but want will perjure
The ne'er touch'd vestal: try thy cunning, Thyreus;
Make thine own edict for thy pains, which we
Will answer as a law.

THYREUS

Caesar, I go.

OCTAVIUS CAESAR

Observe how Antony becomes his flaw,
And what thou think'st his very action speaks
In every power that moves.

THYREUS
  Caesar, I shall.

Exeunt

SCENE XIII.
Alexandria. CLEOPATRA's palace.

Enter CLEOPATRA, DOMITIUS ENOBARBUS, CHARMIAN, and IRAS

CLEOPATRA
  What shall we do, Enobarbus?
DOMITIUS ENOBARBUS
  Think, and die.
CLEOPATRA
  Is Antony or we in fault for this?
DOMITIUS ENOBARBUS
  Antony only, that would make his will
  Lord of his reason. What though you fled
  From that great face of war, whose several ranges
  Frighted each other? why should he follow?
  The itch of his affection should not then
  Have nick'd his captainship; at such a point,
  When half to half the world opposed, he being
  The meered question: 'twas a shame no less
  Than was his loss, to course your flying flags,
  And leave his navy gazing.
CLEOPATRA
  Prithee, peace.

Enter MARK ANTONY with EUPHRONIUS, the Ambassador

MARK ANTONY
  Is that his answer?

EUPHRONIUS
Ay, my lord.
MARK ANTONY
The queen shall then have courtesy, so she
Will yield us up.
EUPHRONIUS
He says so.
MARK ANTONY
Let her know't.
To the boy Caesar send this grizzled head,
And he will fill thy wishes to the brim
With principalities.
CLEOPATRA
That head, my lord?
MARK ANTONY
To him again: tell him he wears the rose
Of youth upon him; from which the world should note
Something particular: his coin, ships, legions,
May be a coward's; whose ministers would prevail
Under the service of a child as soon
As i' the command of Caesar: I dare him therefore
To lay his gay comparisons apart,
And answer me declined, sword against sword,
Ourselves alone. I'll write it: follow me.

Exeunt MARK ANTONY and EUPHRONIUS

DOMITIUS ENOBARBUS
[Aside]
Yes, like enough, high-battled Caesar will
Unstate his happiness, and be staged to the show,
Against a sworder! I see men's judgments are
A parcel of their fortunes; and things outward
Do draw the inward quality after them,
To suffer all alike. That he should dream,

Knowing all measures, the full Caesar will
Answer his emptiness! Caesar, thou hast subdued
His judgment too.

Enter an Attendant

Attendant
A messenger from CAESAR.
CLEOPATRA
What, no more ceremony? See, my women!
Against the blown rose may they stop their nose
That kneel'd unto the buds. Admit him, sir.

Exit Attendant

DOMITIUS ENOBARBUS
[Aside]
Mine honesty and I begin to square.
The loyalty well held to fools does make
Our faith mere folly: yet he that can endure
To follow with allegiance a fall'n lord
Does conquer him that did his master conquer
And earns a place i' the story.

Enter THYREUS

CLEOPATRA
Caesar's will?
THYREUS
Hear it apart.
CLEOPATRA
None but friends: say boldly.
THYREUS
So, haply, are they friends to Antony.
DOMITIUS ENOBARBUS
He needs as many, sir, as Caesar has;

    Or needs not us. If Caesar please, our master
    Will leap to be his friend: for us, you know,
    Whose he is we are, and that is, Caesar's.
THYREUS
    So.
    Thus then, thou most renown'd: Caesar entreats,
    Not to consider in what case thou stand'st,
    Further than he is Caesar.
CLEOPATRA
    Go on: right royal.
THYREUS
    He knows that you embrace not Antony
    As you did love, but as you fear'd him.
CLEOPATRA
    O!
THYREUS
    The scars upon your honour, therefore, he
    Does pity, as constrained blemishes,
    Not as deserved.
CLEOPATRA
    He is a god, and knows
    What is most right: mine honour was not yielded,
    But conquer'd merely.
DOMITIUS ENOBARBUS
          [Aside]
    To be sure of that,
    I will ask Antony. Sir, sir, thou art so leaky,
    That we must leave thee to thy sinking, for
    Thy dearest quit thee.

                Exit

THYREUS
    Shall I say to Caesar

What you require of him? for he partly begs
To be desired to give. It much would please him,
That of his fortunes you should make a staff
To lean upon: but it would warm his spirits,
To hear from me you had left Antony,
And put yourself under his shrowd,
The universal landlord.

CLEOPATRA
What's your name?

THYREUS
My name is Thyreus.

CLEOPATRA
Most kind messenger,
Say to great Caesar this: in deputation
I kiss his conquering hand: tell him, I am prompt
To lay my crown at 's feet, and there to kneel:
Tell him from his all-obeying breath I hear
The doom of Egypt.

THYREUS
'Tis your noblest course.
Wisdom and fortune combating together,
If that the former dare but what it can,
No chance may shake it. Give me grace to lay
My duty on your hand.

CLEOPATRA
Your Caesar's father oft,
When he hath mused of taking kingdoms in,
Bestow'd his lips on that unworthy place,
As it rain'd kisses.

Re-enter MARK ANTONY and DOMITIUS ENOBARBUS

MARK ANTONY
Favours, by Jove that thunders!
What art thou, fellow?

THYREUS
  One that but performs
  The bidding of the fullest man, and worthiest
  To have command obey'd.
DOMITIUS ENOBARBUS
          [Aside]
  You will be whipp'd.
MARK ANTONY
  Approach, there! Ah, you kite! Now, gods
  and devils!
  Authority melts from me: of late, when I cried 'Ho!'
  Like boys unto a muss, kings would start forth,
  And cry 'Your will?' Have you no ears? I am
  Antony yet.
          Enter Attendants
  Take hence this Jack, and whip him.
DOMITIUS ENOBARBUS
          [Aside]
  'Tis better playing with a lion's whelp
  Than with an old one dying.
MARK ANTONY
  Moon and stars!
  Whip him. Were't twenty of the greatest tributaries
  That do acknowledge Caesar, should I find them
  So saucy with the hand of she here,--what's her name,
  Since she was Cleopatra? Whip him, fellows,
  Till, like a boy, you see him cringe his face,
  And whine aloud for mercy: take him hence.
THYREUS
  Mark Antony!
MARK ANTONY
  Tug him away: being whipp'd,
  Bring him again: this Jack of Caesar's shall
  Bear us an errand to him.

Exeunt Attendants with THYREUS
You were half blasted ere I knew you: ha!
Have I my pillow left unpress'd in Rome,
Forborne the getting of a lawful race,
And by a gem of women, to be abused
By one that looks on feeders?

CLEOPATRA
Good my lord,--

MARK ANTONY
You have been a boggler ever:
But when we in our viciousness grow hard--
O misery on't!--the wise gods seel our eyes;
In our own filth drop our clear judgments; make us
Adore our errors; laugh at's, while we strut
To our confusion.

CLEOPATRA
O, is't come to this?

MARK ANTONY
I found you as a morsel cold upon
Dead Caesar's trencher; nay, you were a fragment
Of Cneius Pompey's; besides what hotter hours,
Unregister'd in vulgar fame, you have
Luxuriously pick'd out: for, I am sure,
Though you can guess what temperance should be,
You know not what it is.

CLEOPATRA
Wherefore is this?

MARK ANTONY
To let a fellow that will take rewards
And say 'God quit you!' be familiar with
My playfellow, your hand; this kingly seal
And plighter of high hearts! O, that I were
Upon the hill of Basan, to outroar

The Tragedie of Anthonie and Cleopatra — Act III

   The horned herd! for I have savage cause;
   And to proclaim it civilly, were like
   A halter'd neck which does the hangman thank
   For being yare about him.

Re-enter Attendants with THYREUS

   Is he whipp'd?
First Attendant
   Soundly, my lord.
MARK ANTONY
   Cried he? and begg'd a' pardon?
First Attendant
   He did ask favour.
MARK ANTONY
   If that thy father live, let him repent
   Thou wast not made his daughter; and be thou sorry
   To follow Caesar in his triumph, since
   Thou hast been whipp'd for following him: henceforth
   The white hand of a lady fever thee,
   Shake thou to look on 't. Get thee back to Caesar,
   Tell him thy entertainment: look, thou say
   He makes me angry with him; for he seems
   Proud and disdainful, harping on what I am,
   Not what he knew I was: he makes me angry;
   And at this time most easy 'tis to do't,
   When my good stars, that were my former guides,
   Have empty left their orbs, and shot their fires
   Into the abysm of hell. If he mislike
   My speech and what is done, tell him he has
   Hipparchus, my enfranched bondman, whom
   He may at pleasure whip, or hang, or torture,
   As he shall like, to quit me: urge it thou:
   Hence with thy stripes, begone!

Exit THYREUS

CLEOPATRA
  Have you done yet?
MARK ANTONY
  Alack, our terrene moon
  Is now eclipsed; and it portends alone
  The fall of Antony!
CLEOPATRA
  I must stay his time.
MARK ANTONY
  To flatter Caesar, would you mingle eyes
  With one that ties his points?
CLEOPATRA
  Not know me yet?
MARK ANTONY
  Cold-hearted toward me?
CLEOPATRA
  Ah, dear, if I be so,
  From my cold heart let heaven engender hail,
  And poison it in the source; and the first stone
  Drop in my neck: as it determines, so
  Dissolve my life! The next Caesarion smite!
  Till by degrees the memory of my womb,
  Together with my brave Egyptians all,
  By the discandying of this pelleted storm,
  Lie graveless, till the flies and gnats of Nile
  Have buried them for prey!
MARK ANTONY
  I am satisfied.
  Caesar sits down in Alexandria; where
  I will oppose his fate. Our force by land
  Hath nobly held; our sever'd navy too
  Have knit again, and fleet, threatening most sea-like.
  Where hast thou been, my heart? Dost thou hear, lady?
  If from the field I shall return once more

The Tragedie of Anthonie and Cleopatra — Act III

    To kiss these lips, I will appear in blood;
    I and my sword will earn our chronicle:
    There's hope in't yet.
CLEOPATRA
    That's my brave lord!
MARK ANTONY
    I will be treble-sinew'd, hearted, breathed,
    And fight maliciously: for when mine hours
    Were nice and lucky, men did ransom lives
    Of me for jests; but now I'll set my teeth,
    And send to darkness all that stop me. Come,
    Let's have one other gaudy night: call to me
    All my sad captains; fill our bowls once more;
    Let's mock the midnight bell.
CLEOPATRA
    It is my birth-day:
    I had thought to have held it poor: but, since my lord
    Is Antony again, I will be Cleopatra.
MARK ANTONY
    We will yet do well.
CLEOPATRA
    Call all his noble captains to my lord.
MARK ANTONY
    Do so, we'll speak to them; and to-night I'll force
    The wine peep through their scars. Come on, my queen;
    There's sap in't yet. The next time I do fight,
    I'll make death love me; for I will contend
    Even with his pestilent scythe.

            Exeunt all but DOMITIUS ENOBARBUS

DOMITIUS ENOBARBUS
    Now he'll outstare the lightning. To be furious,
    Is to be frighted out of fear; and in that mood
    The dove will peck the estridge; and I see still,

A diminution in our captain's brain
Restores his heart: when valour preys on reason,
It eats the sword it fights with. I will seek
Some way to leave him.

Exit

ACT IV

SCENE I.
Before Alexandria. OCTAVIUS CAESAR's camp.

Enter OCTAVIUS CAESAR, AGRIPPA, and MECAENAS, with his Army; OCTAVIUS CAESAR reading a letter

OCTAVIUS CAESAR
    He calls me boy; and chides, as he had power
    To beat me out of Egypt; my messenger
    He hath whipp'd with rods; dares me to personal combat,
    Caesar to Antony: let the old ruffian know
    I have many other ways to die; meantime
    Laugh at his challenge.
MECAENAS
    Caesar must think,
    When one so great begins to rage, he's hunted
    Even to falling. Give him no breath, but now
    Make boot of his distraction: never anger
    Made good guard for itself.
OCTAVIUS CAESAR
    Let our best heads
    Know, that to-morrow the last of many battles
    We mean to fight: within our files there are,
    Of those that served Mark Antony but late,
    Enough to fetch him in. See it done:
    And feast the army; we have store to do't,
    And they have earn'd the waste. Poor Antony!

Exeunt

The Tragedie of Anthonie and Cleopatra — Act IV

SCENE II.
Alexandria. CLEOPATRA's palace.

Enter MARK ANTONY, CLEOPATRA, DOMITIUS ENOBARBUS, CHARMIAN, IRAS, ALEXAS, with others

MARK ANTONY
  He will not fight with me, Domitius.
DOMITIUS ENOBARBUS
  No.
MARK ANTONY
  Why should he not?
DOMITIUS ENOBARBUS
  He thinks, being twenty times of better fortune,
  He is twenty men to one.
MARK ANTONY
  To-morrow, soldier,
  By sea and land I'll fight: or I will live,
  Or bathe my dying honour in the blood
  Shall make it live again. Woo't thou fight well?
DOMITIUS ENOBARBUS
  I'll strike, and cry 'Take all.'
MARK ANTONY
  Well said; come on.
  Call forth my household servants: let's to-night
  Be bounteous at our meal.

Enter three or four Servitors

  Give me thy hand,
  Thou hast been rightly honest;--so hast thou;--
  Thou,--and thou,--and thou:--you have served me well,
  And kings have been your fellows.
CLEOPATRA
            [Aside to DOMITIUS ENOBARBUS]
  What means this?

The Tragedie of Anthonie and Cleopatra — Act IV

DOMITIUS ENOBARBUS
> *[Aside to CLEOPATRA].*

'Tis one of those odd
tricks which sorrow shoots
Out of the mind.

MARK ANTONY

And thou art honest too.
I wish I could be made so many men,
And all of you clapp'd up together in
An Antony, that I might do you service
So good as you have done.

All

The gods forbid!

MARK ANTONY

Well, my good fellows, wait on me to-night:
Scant not my cups; and make as much of me
As when mine empire was your fellow too,
And suffer'd my command.

CLEOPATRA
> *[Aside to DOMITIUS ENOBARBUS]*

What does he mean?

DOMITIUS ENOBARBUS
> *[Aside to CLEOPATRA]*

To make his followers weep.

MARK ANTONY

Tend me to-night;
May be it is the period of your duty:
Haply you shall not see me more; or if,
A mangled shadow: perchance to-morrow
You'll serve another master. I look on you
As one that takes his leave. Mine honest friends,
I turn you not away; but, like a master
Married to your good service, stay till death:
Tend me to-night two hours, I ask no more,

    And the gods yield you for't!
DOMITIUS ENOBARBUS
    What mean you, sir,
    To give them this discomfort? Look, they weep;
    And I, an ass, am onion-eyed: for shame,
    Transform us not to women.
MARK ANTONY
    Ho, ho, ho!
    Now the witch take me, if I meant it thus!
    Grace grow where those drops fall!
    My hearty friends,
    You take me in too dolorous a sense;
    For I spake to you for your comfort; did desire you
    To burn this night with torches: know, my hearts,
    I hope well of to-morrow; and will lead you
    Where rather I'll expect victorious life
    Than death and honour. Let's to supper, come,
    And drown consideration.

Exeunt

SCENE III.
The same. Before the palace.

Enter two Soldiers to their guard

First Soldier
    Brother, good night: to-morrow is the day.
Second Soldier
    It will determine one way: fare you well.
    Heard you of nothing strange about the streets?
First Soldier
    Nothing. What news?

The Tragedie of Anthonie and Cleopatra — Act IV

Second Soldier
  Belike 'tis but a rumour. Good night to you.
First Soldier
  Well, sir, good night.

Enter two other Soldiers

Second Soldier
  Soldiers, have careful watch.
Third Soldier
  And you. Good night, good night.

They place themselves in every corner of the stage

Fourth Soldier
  Here we: and if to-morrow
  Our navy thrive, I have an absolute hope
  Our landmen will stand up.
Third Soldier
  'Tis a brave army,
  And full of purpose.

Music of the hautboys as under the stage

Fourth Soldier
  Peace! what noise?
First Soldier
  List, list!
Second Soldier
  Hark!
First Soldier
  Music i' the air.
Third Soldier
  Under the earth.
Fourth Soldier
  It signs well, does it not?

Third Soldier
  No.
First Soldier
  Peace, I say!
  What should this mean?
Second Soldier
  'Tis the god Hercules, whom Antony loved,
  Now leaves him.
First Soldier
  Walk; let's see if other watchmen
  Do hear what we do?

> *They advance to another post*

Second Soldier
  How now, masters!
All
     [Speaking together]
  How now!
  How now! do you hear this?
First Soldier
  Ay; is't not strange?
Third Soldier
  Do you hear, masters? do you hear?
First Soldier
  Follow the noise so far as we have quarter;
  Let's see how it will give off.
All
  Content. 'Tis strange.

> *Exeunt*

The Tragedie of Anthonie and Cleopatra — Act IV

SCENE IV.
The same. A room in the palace.

Enter MARK ANTONY and CLEOPATRA, CHARMIAN, and others attending

MARK ANTONY
 Eros! mine armour, Eros!
CLEOPATRA
 Sleep a little.
MARK ANTONY
 No, my chuck. Eros, come; mine armour, Eros!

Enter EROS with armour

 Come good fellow, put mine iron on:
 If fortune be not ours to-day, it is
 Because we brave her: come.
CLEOPATRA
 Nay, I'll help too.
 What's this for?
MARK ANTONY
 Ah, let be, let be! thou art
 The armourer of my heart: false, false; this, this.
CLEOPATRA
 Sooth, la, I'll help: thus it must be.
MARK ANTONY
 Well, well;
 We shall thrive now. Seest thou, my good fellow?
 Go put on thy defences.
EROS
 Briefly, sir.
CLEOPATRA
 Is not this buckled well?
MARK ANTONY
 Rarely, rarely:

He that unbuckles this, till we do please
To daff't for our repose, shall hear a storm.
Thou fumblest, Eros; and my queen's a squire
More tight at this than thou: dispatch. O love,
That thou couldst see my wars to-day, and knew'st
The royal occupation! thou shouldst see
A workman in't.

Enter an armed Soldier

Good morrow to thee; welcome:
Thou look'st like him that knows a warlike charge:
To business that we love we rise betime,
And go to't with delight.

Soldier
  A thousand, sir,
  Early though't be, have on their riveted trim,
  And at the port expect you.

Shout. Trumpets flourish

Enter Captains and Soldiers

Captain
  The morn is fair. Good morrow, general.
All
  Good morrow, general.
MARK ANTONY
  'Tis well blown, lads:
  This morning, like the spirit of a youth
  That means to be of note, begins betimes.
  So, so; come, give me that: this way; well said.
  Fare thee well, dame, whate'er becomes of me:
  This is a soldier's kiss: rebukeable

Kisses her

And worthy shameful cheque it were, to stand

On more mechanic compliment; I'll leave thee
Now, like a man of steel. You that will fight,
Follow me close; I'll bring you to't. Adieu.

Exeunt MARK ANTONY, EROS, Captains, and Soldiers

CHARMIAN
Please you, retire to your chamber.
CLEOPATRA
Lead me.
He goes forth gallantly. That he and Caesar might
Determine this great war in single fight!
Then Antony,--but now--Well, on.

Exeunt

SCENE V.
Alexandria. MARK ANTONY's camp.

Trumpets sound. Enter MARK ANTONY and EROS; a Soldier meeting them

Soldier
The gods make this a happy day to Antony!
MARK ANTONY
Would thou and those thy scars had once prevail'd
To make me fight at land!
Soldier
Hadst thou done so,
The kings that have revolted, and the soldier
That has this morning left thee, would have still
Follow'd thy heels.
MARK ANTONY
Who's gone this morning?

The Tragedie of Anthonie and Cleopatra — Act IV

Soldier
  Who!
  One ever near thee: call for Enobarbus,
  He shall not hear thee; or from Caesar's camp
  Say 'I am none of thine.'
MARK ANTONY
  What say'st thou?
Soldier
  Sir,
  He is with Caesar.
EROS
  Sir, his chests and treasure
  He has not with him.
MARK ANTONY
  Is he gone?
Soldier
  Most certain.
MARK ANTONY
  Go, Eros, send his treasure after; do it;
  Detain no jot, I charge thee: write to him--
  I will subscribe--gentle adieus and greetings;
  Say that I wish he never find more cause
  To change a master. O, my fortunes have
  Corrupted honest men! Dispatch.--Enobarbus!

Exeunt

The Tragedie of Anthonie and Cleopatra — Act IV

SCENE VI.
Alexandria. OCTAVIUS CAESAR's camp.

Flourish. Enter OCTAVIUS CAESAR, AGRIPPA, with DOMITIUS ENOBARBUS, and others

OCTAVIUS CAESAR
 Go forth, Agrippa, and begin the fight:
 Our will is Antony be took alive;
 Make it so known.
AGRIPPA
 Caesar, I shall.

Exit

OCTAVIUS CAESAR
 The time of universal peace is near:
 Prove this a prosperous day, the three-nook'd world
 Shall bear the olive freely.

Enter a Messenger

Messenger
 Antony
 Is come into the field.
OCTAVIUS CAESAR
 Go charge Agrippa
 Plant those that have revolted in the van,
 That Antony may seem to spend his fury
 Upon himself.

Exeunt all but DOMITIUS ENOBARBUS

DOMITIUS ENOBARBUS
 Alexas did revolt; and went to Jewry on
 Affairs of Antony; there did persuade

Great Herod to incline himself to Caesar,
And leave his master Antony: for this pains
Caesar hath hang'd him. Canidius and the rest
That fell away have entertainment, but
No honourable trust. I have done ill;
Of which I do accuse myself so sorely,
That I will joy no more.

Enter a Soldier of CAESAR's

Soldier
　Enobarbus, Antony
　Hath after thee sent all thy treasure, with
　His bounty overplus: the messenger
　Came on my guard; and at thy tent is now
　Unloading of his mules.
DOMITIUS ENOBARBUS
　I give it you.
Soldier
　Mock not, Enobarbus.
　I tell you true: best you safed the bringer
　Out of the host; I must attend mine office,
　Or would have done't myself. Your emperor
　Continues still a Jove.

Exit

DOMITIUS ENOBARBUS
　I am alone the villain of the earth,
　And feel I am so most. O Antony,
　Thou mine of bounty, how wouldst thou have paid
　My better service, when my turpitude
　Thou dost so crown with gold! This blows my heart:
　If swift thought break it not, a swifter mean
　Shall outstrike thought: but thought will do't, I feel.

I fight against thee! No: I will go seek
Some ditch wherein to die; the foul'st best fits
My latter part of life.

Exit

SCENE VII.
Field of battle between the camps.

Alarum. Drums and trumpets. Enter AGRIPPA and others

AGRIPPA
Retire, we have engaged ourselves too far:
Caesar himself has work, and our oppression
Exceeds what we expected.

Exeunt

Alarums. Enter MARK ANTONY and SCARUS wounded

SCARUS
O my brave emperor, this is fought indeed!
Had we done so at first, we had droven them home
With clouts about their heads.
MARK ANTONY
Thou bleed'st apace.
SCARUS
I had a wound here that was like a T,
But now 'tis made an H.
MARK ANTONY
They do retire.
SCARUS
We'll beat 'em into bench-holes: I have yet
Room for six scotches more.

The Tragedie of Anthonie and Cleopatra — Act IV

Enter EROS

EROS
   They are beaten, sir, and our advantage serves
   For a fair victory.
SCARUS
   Let us score their backs,
   And snatch 'em up, as we take hares, behind:
   'Tis sport to maul a runner.
MARK ANTONY
   I will reward thee
   Once for thy spritely comfort, and ten-fold
   For thy good valour. Come thee on.
SCARUS
   I'll halt after.

Exeunt

SCENE VIII.
Under the walls of Alexandria.

Alarum. Enter MARK ANTONY, in a march; SCARUS, with others

MARK ANTONY
   We have beat him to his camp: run one before,
   And let the queen know of our gests. To-morrow,
   Before the sun shall see 's, we'll spill the blood
   That has to-day escaped. I thank you all;
   For doughty-handed are you, and have fought
   Not as you served the cause, but as 't had been
   Each man's like mine; you have shown all Hectors.
   Enter the city, clip your wives, your friends,
   Tell them your feats; whilst they with joyful tears

The Tragedie of Anthonie and Cleopatra — Act IV

Wash the congealment from your wounds, and kiss
The honour'd gashes whole.
> *To SCARUS*

Give me thy hand

> *Enter CLEOPATRA, attended*

To this great fairy I'll commend thy acts,
Make her thanks bless thee.
> *To CLEOPATRA*

O thou day o' the world,
Chain mine arm'd neck; leap thou, attire and all,
Through proof of harness to my heart, and there
Ride on the pants triumphing!

CLEOPATRA
Lord of lords!
O infinite virtue, comest thou smiling from
The world's great snare uncaught?

MARK ANTONY
My nightingale,
We have beat them to their beds. What, girl!
though grey
Do something mingle with our younger brown, yet ha' we
A brain that nourishes our nerves, and can
Get goal for goal of youth. Behold this man;
Commend unto his lips thy favouring hand:
Kiss it, my warrior: he hath fought to-day
As if a god, in hate of mankind, had
Destroy'd in such a shape.

CLEOPATRA
I'll give thee, friend,
An armour all of gold; it was a king's.

MARK ANTONY
He has deserved it, were it carbuncled
Like holy Phoebus' car. Give me thy hand:
Through Alexandria make a jolly march;

The Tragedie of Anthonie and Cleopatra — Act IV

Bear our hack'd targets like the men that owe them:
Had our great palace the capacity
To camp this host, we all would sup together,
And drink carouses to the next day's fate,
Which promises royal peril. Trumpeters,
With brazen din blast you the city's ear;
Make mingle with rattling tabourines;
That heaven and earth may strike their sounds together,
Applauding our approach.

Exeunt

SCENE IX.
OCTAVIUS CAESAR's camp.

Sentinels at their post

First Soldier
   If we be not relieved within this hour,
   We must return to the court of guard: the night
   Is shiny; and they say we shall embattle
   By the second hour i' the morn.
Second Soldier
   This last day was
   A shrewd one to's.

Enter DOMITIUS ENOBARBUS

DOMITIUS ENOBARBUS
   O, bear me witness, night,--
Third Soldier
   What man is this?
Second Soldier
   Stand close, and list him.

The Tragedie of Anthonie and Cleopatra — Act IV

DOMITIUS ENOBARBUS
   Be witness to me, O thou blessed moon,
   When men revolted shall upon record
   Bear hateful memory, poor Enobarbus did
   Before thy face repent!
First Soldier
   Enobarbus!
Third Soldier
   Peace!
   Hark further.
DOMITIUS ENOBARBUS
   O sovereign mistress of true melancholy,
   The poisonous damp of night disponge upon me,
   That life, a very rebel to my will,
   May hang no longer on me: throw my heart
   Against the flint and hardness of my fault:
   Which, being dried with grief, will break to powder,
   And finish all foul thoughts. O Antony,
   Nobler than my revolt is infamous,
   Forgive me in thine own particular;
   But let the world rank me in register
   A master-leaver and a fugitive:
   O Antony! O Antony!

Dies

Second Soldier
   Let's speak To him.
First Soldier
   Let's hear him, for the things he speaks
   May concern Caesar.
Third Soldier
   Let's do so. But he sleeps.
First Soldier
   Swoons rather; for so bad a prayer as his

Was never yet for sleep.
Second Soldier
Go we to him.
Third Soldier
Awake, sir, awake; speak to us.
Second Soldier
Hear you, sir?
First Soldier
The hand of death hath raught him.

Drums afar off

Hark! the drums
Demurely wake the sleepers. Let us bear him
To the court of guard; he is of note: our hour
Is fully out.
Third Soldier
Come on, then;
He may recover yet.

Exeunt with the body

SCENE X.
Between the two camps.

Enter MARK ANTONY and SCARUS, with their Army

MARK ANTONY
Their preparation is to-day by sea;
We please them not by land.
SCARUS
For both, my lord.
MARK ANTONY
I would they'ld fight i' the fire or i' the air;
We'ld fight there too. But this it is; our foot
Upon the hills adjoining to the city

Shall stay with us: order for sea is given;
They have put forth the haven
Where their appointment we may best discover,
And look on their endeavour.

Exeunt

SCENE XI.
Another part of the same.

Enter OCTAVIUS CAESAR, and his Army

OCTAVIUS CAESAR
But being charged, we will be still by land,
Which, as I take't, we shall; for his best force
Is forth to man his galleys. To the vales,
And hold our best advantage.

Exeunt

SCENE XII.
Another part of the same.

Enter MARK ANTONY and SCARUS

MARK ANTONY
Yet they are not join'd: where yond pine
does stand,
I shall discover all: I'll bring thee word
Straight, how 'tis like to go.

Exit

SCARUS
Swallows have built

The Tragedie of Anthonie and Cleopatra — Act IV

In Cleopatra's sails their nests: the augurers
Say they know not, they cannot tell; look grimly,
And dare not speak their knowledge. Antony
Is valiant, and dejected; and, by starts,
His fretted fortunes give him hope, and fear,
Of what he has, and has not.

Alarum afar off, as at a sea-fight

Re-enter MARK ANTONY

MARK ANTONY
All is lost;
This foul Egyptian hath betrayed me:
My fleet hath yielded to the foe; and yonder
They cast their caps up and carouse together
Like friends long lost. Triple-turn'd whore!
'tis thou
Hast sold me to this novice; and my heart
Makes only wars on thee. Bid them all fly;
For when I am revenged upon my charm,
I have done all. Bid them all fly; begone.

Exit SCARUS

O sun, thy uprise shall I see no more:
Fortune and Antony part here; even here
Do we shake hands. All come to this? The hearts
That spaniel'd me at heels, to whom I gave
Their wishes, do discandy, melt their sweets
On blossoming Caesar; and this pine is bark'd,
That overtopp'd them all. Betray'd I am:
O this false soul of Egypt! this grave charm,--
Whose eye beck'd forth my wars, and call'd them home;
Whose bosom was my crownet, my chief end,--
Like a right gipsy, hath, at fast and loose,

The Tragedie of Anthonie and Cleopatra — Act IV

Beguiled me to the very heart of loss.
What, Eros, Eros!

Enter CLEOPATRA

Ah, thou spell! Avaunt!
CLEOPATRA
Why is my lord enraged against his love?
MARK ANTONY
Vanish, or I shall give thee thy deserving,
And blemish Caesar's triumph. Let him take thee,
And hoist thee up to the shouting plebeians:
Follow his chariot, like the greatest spot
Of all thy sex; most monster-like, be shown
For poor'st diminutives, for doits; and let
Patient Octavia plough thy visage up
With her prepared nails.

Exit CLEOPATRA

'Tis well thou'rt gone,
If it be well to live; but better 'twere
Thou fell'st into my fury, for one death
Might have prevented many. Eros, ho!
The shirt of Nessus is upon me: teach me,
Alcides, thou mine ancestor, thy rage:
Let me lodge Lichas on the horns o' the moon;
And with those hands, that grasp'd the heaviest club,
Subdue my worthiest self. The witch shall die:
To the young Roman boy she hath sold me, and I fall
Under this plot; she dies for't. Eros, ho!

Exit

The Tragedie of Anthonie and Cleopatra — Act IV

SCENE XIII.
Alexandria. Cleopatra's palace.

Enter CLEOPATRA, CHARMIAN, IRAS, and MARDIAN

CLEOPATRA
  Help me, my women! O, he is more mad
  Than Telamon for his shield; the boar of Thessaly
  Was never so emboss'd.
CHARMIAN
  To the monument!
  There lock yourself, and send him word you are dead.
  The soul and body rive not more in parting
  Than greatness going off.
CLEOPATRA
  To the monument!
  Mardian, go tell him I have slain myself;
  Say, that the last I spoke was 'Antony,'
  And word it, prithee, piteously: hence, Mardian,
  And bring me how he takes my death.
  To the monument!

Exeunt

SCENE XIV.
The same. Another room.

Enter MARK ANTONY and EROS

MARK ANTONY
  Eros, thou yet behold'st me?
EROS
  Ay, noble lord.

The Tragedie of Anthonie and Cleopatra — Act IV

MARK ANTONY
  Sometimes we see a cloud that's dragonish;
  A vapour sometime like a bear or lion,
  A tower'd citadel, a pendent rock,
  A forked mountain, or blue promontory
  With trees upon't, that nod unto the world,
  And mock our eyes with air: thou hast seen
  these signs;
  They are black vesper's pageants.
EROS
  Ay, my lord,
MARK ANTONY
  That which is now a horse, even with a thought
  The rack dislimns, and makes it indistinct,
  As water is in water.
EROS
  It does, my lord.
MARK ANTONY
  My good knave Eros, now thy captain is
  Even such a body: here I am Antony:
  Yet cannot hold this visible shape, my knave.
  I made these wars for Egypt: and the queen,--
  Whose heart I thought I had, for she had mine;
  Which whilst it was mine had annex'd unto't
  A million more, now lost,--she, Eros, has
  Pack'd cards with Caesar, and false-play'd my glory
  Unto an enemy's triumph.
  Nay, weep not, gentle Eros; there is left us
  Ourselves to end ourselves.

                Enter MARDIAN

  O! thy vile lady!
  She has robb'd me of my sword.
MARDIAN

The Tragedie of Anthonie and Cleopatra — Act IV

    No, Antony;
    My mistress loved thee, and her fortunes mingled
    With thine entirely.

MARK ANTONY
    Hence, saucy eunuch; peace!
    She hath betray'd me and shall die the death.

MARDIAN
    Death of one person can be paid but once,
    And that she has discharged: what thou wouldst do
    Is done unto thy hand: the last she spake
    Was 'Antony! most noble Antony!'
    Then in the midst a tearing groan did break
    The name of Antony; it was divided
    Between her heart and lips: she render'd life,
    Thy name so buried in her.

MARK ANTONY
    Dead, then?

MARDIAN
    Dead.

MARK ANTONY
    Unarm, Eros; the long day's task is done,
    And we must sleep.
          To MARDIAN
    That thou depart'st hence safe,
    Does pay thy labour richly; go.

          Exit MARDIAN

    Off, pluck off:
    The seven-fold shield of Ajax cannot keep
    The battery from my heart. O, cleave, my sides!
    Heart, once be stronger than thy continent,
    Crack thy frail case! Apace, Eros, apace.
    No more a soldier: bruised pieces, go;
    You have been nobly borne. From me awhile.

The Tragedie of Anthonie and Cleopatra — Act IV

Exit EROS

I will o'ertake thee, Cleopatra, and
Weep for my pardon. So it must be, for now
All length is torture: since the torch is out,
Lie down, and stray no farther: now all labour
Mars what it does; yea, very force entangles
Itself with strength: seal then, and all is done.
Eros!--I come, my queen:--Eros!--Stay for me:
Where souls do couch on flowers, we'll hand in hand,
And with our sprightly port make the ghosts gaze:
Dido and her AEneas shall want troops,
And all the haunt be ours. Come, Eros, Eros!

Re-enter EROS

EROS
   What would my lord?
MARK ANTONY
   Since Cleopatra died,
   I have lived in such dishonour, that the gods
   Detest my baseness. I, that with my sword
   Quarter'd the world, and o'er green Neptune's back
   With ships made cities, condemn myself to lack
   The courage of a woman; less noble mind
   Than she which by her death our Caesar tells
   'I am conqueror of myself.' Thou art sworn, Eros,
   That, when the exigent should come, which now
   Is come indeed, when I should see behind me
   The inevitable prosecution of
   Disgrace and horror, that, on my command,
   Thou then wouldst kill me: do't; the time is come:
   Thou strikest not me, 'tis Caesar thou defeat'st.
   Put colour in thy cheek.
EROS
   The gods withhold me!

> Shall I do that which all the Parthian darts,
> Though enemy, lost aim, and could not?

MARK ANTONY
> Eros,
> Wouldst thou be window'd in great Rome and see
> Thy master thus with pleach'd arms, bending down
> His corrigible neck, his face subdued
> To penetrative shame, whilst the wheel'd seat
> Of fortunate Caesar, drawn before him, branded
> His baseness that ensued?

EROS
> I would not see't.

MARK ANTONY
> Come, then; for with a wound I must be cured.
> Draw that thy honest sword, which thou hast worn
> Most useful for thy country.

EROS
> O, sir, pardon me!

MARK ANTONY
> When I did make thee free, sworest thou not then
> To do this when I bade thee? Do it at once;
> Or thy precedent services are all
> But accidents unpurposed. Draw, and come.

EROS
> Turn from me, then, that noble countenance,
> Wherein the worship of the whole world lies.

MARK ANTONY
> Lo thee!

Turning from him

EROS
> My sword is drawn.

MARK ANTONY
> Then let it do at once

The Tragedie of Anthonie and Cleopatra — Act IV

    The thing why thou hast drawn it.
EROS
    My dear master,
    My captain, and my emperor, let me say,
    Before I strike this bloody stroke, farewell.
MARK ANTONY
    'Tis said, man; and farewell.
EROS
    Farewell, great chief. Shall I strike now?
MARK ANTONY
    Now, Eros.
EROS
    Why, there then: thus I do escape the sorrow
    Of Antony's death.

Kills himself

MARK ANTONY
    Thrice-nobler than myself!
    Thou teachest me, O valiant Eros, what
    I should, and thou couldst not. My queen and Eros
    Have by their brave instruction got upon me
    A nobleness in record: but I will be
    A bridegroom in my death, and run into't
    As to a lover's bed. Come, then; and, Eros,
    Thy master dies thy scholar: to do thus

Falling on his sword

    I learn'd of thee. How! not dead? not dead?
    The guard, ho! O, dispatch me!

Enter DERCETAS and Guard

First Guard
    What's the noise?

The Tragedie of Anthonie and Cleopatra — Act IV

MARK ANTONY
  I have done my work in, friends: O, make an end
  Of what I have begun.
Second Guard
  The star is fall'n.
First Guard
  And time is at his period.
All
  Alas, and woe!
MARK ANTONY
  Let him that loves me strike me dead.
First Guard
  Not I.
Second Guard
  Nor I.
Third Guard
  Nor any one.

Exeunt Guard

DERCETAS
  Thy death and fortunes bid thy followers fly.
  This sword but shown to Caesar, with this tidings,
  Shall enter me with him.

Enter DIOMEDES

DIOMEDES
  Where's Antony?
DERCETAS
  There, Diomed there.
DIOMEDES
  Lives he?
  Wilt thou not answer, man?

The Tragedie of Anthonie and Cleopatra — Act IV

Exit DERCETAS

MARK ANTONY
  Art thou there, Diomed? Draw thy sword, and give me
  Sufficing strokes for death.
DIOMEDES
  Most absolute lord,
  My mistress Cleopatra sent me to thee.
MARK ANTONY
  When did she send thee?
DIOMEDES
  Now, my lord.
MARK ANTONY
  Where is she?
DIOMEDES
  Lock'd in her monument. She had a prophesying fear
  Of what hath come to pass: for when she saw--
  Which never shall be found--you did suspect
  She had disposed with Caesar, and that your rage
  Would not be purged, she sent you word she was dead;
  But, fearing since how it might work, hath sent
  Me to proclaim the truth; and I am come,
  I dread, too late.
MARK ANTONY
  Too late, good Diomed: call my guard, I prithee.
DIOMEDES
  What, ho, the emperor's guard! The guard, what, ho!
  Come, your lord calls!

  Enter four or five of the Guard of MARK ANTONY

MARK ANTONY
  Bear me, good friends, where Cleopatra bides;
  'Tis the last service that I shall command you.

First Guard
   Woe, woe are we, sir, you may not live to wear
   All your true followers out.
All
   Most heavy day!
MARK ANTONY
   Nay, good my fellows, do not please sharp fate
   To grace it with your sorrows: bid that welcome
   Which comes to punish us, and we punish it
   Seeming to bear it lightly. Take me up:
   I have led you oft: carry me now, good friends,
   And have my thanks for all.

> *Exeunt, bearing MARK ANTONY*

SCENE XV.
The same. A monument.

Enter CLEOPATRA and her maids aloft, with CHARMIAN and IRAS

CLEOPATRA
   O Charmian, I will never go from hence.
CHARMIAN
   Be comforted, dear madam.
CLEOPATRA
   No, I will not:
   All strange and terrible events are welcome,
   But comforts we despise; our size of sorrow,
   Proportion'd to our cause, must be as great
   As that which makes it.

> *Enter, below, DIOMEDES*

   How now! is he dead?

The Tragedie of Anthonie and Cleopatra — Act IV

DIOMEDES
His death's upon him, but not dead.
Look out o' the other side your monument;
His guard have brought him thither.

Enter, below, MARK ANTONY, borne by the Guard

CLEOPATRA
O sun,
Burn the great sphere thou movest in!
darkling stand
The varying shore o' the world. O Antony,
Antony, Antony! Help, Charmian, help, Iras, help;
Help, friends below; let's draw him hither.

MARK ANTONY
Peace!
Not Caesar's valour hath o'erthrown Antony,
But Antony's hath triumph'd on itself.

CLEOPATRA
So it should be, that none but Antony
Should conquer Antony; but woe 'tis so!

MARK ANTONY
I am dying, Egypt, dying; only
I here importune death awhile, until
Of many thousand kisses the poor last
I lay up thy lips.

CLEOPATRA
I dare not, dear,--
Dear my lord, pardon,--I dare not,
Lest I be taken: not the imperious show
Of the full-fortuned Caesar ever shall
Be brooch'd with me; if knife, drugs,
serpents, have
Edge, sting, or operation, I am safe:
Your wife Octavia, with her modest eyes

The Tragedie of Anthonie and Cleopatra — Act IV

   And still conclusion, shall acquire no honour
   Demuring upon me. But come, come, Antony,--
   Help me, my women,--we must draw thee up:
   Assist, good friends.

MARK ANTONY
   O, quick, or I am gone.

CLEOPATRA
   Here's sport indeed! How heavy weighs my lord!
   Our strength is all gone into heaviness,
   That makes the weight: had I great Juno's power,
   The strong-wing'd Mercury should fetch thee up,
   And set thee by Jove's side. Yet come a little,--
   Wishes were ever fools,--O, come, come, come;

      They heave MARK ANTONY aloft to CLEOPATRA

   And welcome, welcome! die where thou hast lived:
   Quicken with kissing: had my lips that power,
   Thus would I wear them out.

All
   A heavy sight!

MARK ANTONY
   I am dying, Egypt, dying:
   Give me some wine, and let me speak a little.

CLEOPATRA
   No, let me speak; and let me rail so high,
   That the false housewife Fortune break her wheel,
   Provoked by my offence.

MARK ANTONY
   One word, sweet queen:
   Of Caesar seek your honour, with your safety. O!

CLEOPATRA
   They do not go together.

MARK ANTONY
   Gentle, hear me:
   None about Caesar trust but Proculeius.

The Tragedie of Anthonie and Cleopatra — Act IV

CLEOPATRA
My resolution and my hands I'll trust;
None about Caesar.

MARK ANTONY
The miserable change now at my end
Lament nor sorrow at; but please your thoughts
In feeding them with those my former fortunes
Wherein I lived, the greatest prince o' the world,
The noblest; and do now not basely die,
Not cowardly put off my helmet to
My countryman,--a Roman by a Roman
Valiantly vanquish'd. Now my spirit is going;
I can no more.

CLEOPATRA
Noblest of men, woo't die?
Hast thou no care of me? shall I abide
In this dull world, which in thy absence is
No better than a sty? O, see, my women,

MARK ANTONY dies

The crown o' the earth doth melt. My lord!
O, wither'd is the garland of the war,
The soldier's pole is fall'n: young boys and girls
Are level now with men; the odds is gone,
And there is nothing left remarkable
Beneath the visiting moon.

Faints

CHARMIAN
O, quietness, lady!

IRAS
She is dead too, our sovereign.

CHARMIAN
Lady!

The Tragedie of Anthonie and Cleopatra — Act IV

IRAS
  Madam!
CHARMIAN
  O madam, madam, madam!
IRAS
  Royal Egypt, Empress!
CHARMIAN
  Peace, peace, Iras!
CLEOPATRA
  No more, but e'en a woman, and commanded
  By such poor passion as the maid that milks
  And does the meanest chares. It were for me
  To throw my sceptre at the injurious gods;
  To tell them that this world did equal theirs
  Till they had stol'n our jewel. All's but naught;
  Patience is scottish, and impatience does
  Become a dog that's mad: then is it sin
  To rush into the secret house of death,
  Ere death dare come to us? How do you, women?
  What, what! good cheer! Why, how now, Charmian!
  My noble girls! Ah, women, women, look,
  Our lamp is spent, it's out! Good sirs, take heart:
  We'll bury him; and then, what's brave,
  what's noble,
  Let's do it after the high Roman fashion,
  And make death proud to take us. Come, away:
  This case of that huge spirit now is cold:
  Ah, women, women! come; we have no friend
  But resolution, and the briefest end.

  Exeunt; those above bearing off MARK ANTONY's body

ACT V

SCENE I.
Alexandria. OCTAVIUS CAESAR's camp.

Enter OCTAVIUS CAESAR, AGRIPPA, DOLABELLA, MECAENAS, GALLUS, PROCULEIUS, and others, his council of war

OCTAVIUS CAESAR
  Go to him, Dolabella, bid him yield;
  Being so frustrate, tell him he mocks
  The pauses that he makes.
DOLABELLA
  Caesar, I shall.

Exit

Enter DERCETAS, with the sword of MARK ANTONY

OCTAVIUS CAESAR
  Wherefore is that? and what art thou that darest
  Appear thus to us?
DERCETAS
  I am call'd Dercetas;
  Mark Antony I served, who best was worthy
  Best to be served: whilst he stood up and spoke,
  He was my master; and I wore my life
  To spend upon his haters. If thou please
  To take me to thee, as I was to him
  I'll be to Caesar; if thou pleasest not,
  I yield thee up my life.

OCTAVIUS CAESAR
  What is't thou say'st?
DERCETAS
  I say, O Caesar, Antony is dead.
OCTAVIUS CAESAR
  The breaking of so great a thing should make
  A greater crack: the round world
  Should have shook lions into civil streets,
  And citizens to their dens: the death of Antony
  Is not a single doom; in the name lay
  A moiety of the world.
DERCETAS
  He is dead, Caesar:
  Not by a public minister of justice,
  Nor by a hired knife; but that self hand,
  Which writ his honour in the acts it did,
  Hath, with the courage which the heart did lend it,
  Splitted the heart. This is his sword;
  I robb'd his wound of it; behold it stain'd
  With his most noble blood.
OCTAVIUS CAESAR
  Look you sad, friends?
  The gods rebuke me, but it is tidings
  To wash the eyes of kings.
AGRIPPA
  And strange it is,
  That nature must compel us to lament
  Our most persisted deeds.
MECAENAS
  His taints and honours
  Waged equal with him.
AGRIPPA
  A rarer spirit never
  Did steer humanity: but you, gods, will give us

The Tragedie of Anthonie and Cleopatra — Act V

   Some faults to make us men. Caesar is touch'd.
MECAENAS
   When such a spacious mirror's set before him,
   He needs must see himself.
OCTAVIUS CAESAR
   O Antony!
   I have follow'd thee to this; but we do lance
   Diseases in our bodies: I must perforce
   Have shown to thee such a declining day,
   Or look on thine; we could not stall together
   In the whole world: but yet let me lament,
   With tears as sovereign as the blood of hearts,
   That thou, my brother, my competitor
   In top of all design, my mate in empire,
   Friend and companion in the front of war,
   The arm of mine own body, and the heart
   Where mine his thoughts did kindle,--that our stars,
   Unreconciliable, should divide
   Our equalness to this. Hear me, good friends--
   But I will tell you at some meeter season:

               Enter an Egyptian

   The business of this man looks out of him;
   We'll hear him what he says. Whence are you?
Egyptian
   A poor Egyptian yet. The queen my mistress,
   Confined in all she has, her monument,
   Of thy intents desires instruction,
   That she preparedly may frame herself
   To the way she's forced to.
OCTAVIUS CAESAR
   Bid her have good heart:
   She soon shall know of us, by some of ours,
   How honourable and how kindly we
   Determine for her; for Caesar cannot live

The Tragedie of Anthonie and Cleopatra — Act V

    To be ungentle.
Egyptian
    So the gods preserve thee!

Exit

OCTAVIUS CAESAR
    Come hither, Proculeius. Go and say,
    We purpose her no shame: give her what comforts
    The quality of her passion shall require,
    Lest, in her greatness, by some mortal stroke
    She do defeat us; for her life in Rome
    Would be eternal in our triumph: go,
    And with your speediest bring us what she says,
    And how you find of her.
PROCULEIUS
    Caesar, I shall.

Exit

OCTAVIUS CAESAR
    Gallus, go you along.

Exit GALLUS

    Where's Dolabella,
    To second Proculeius?
All
    Dolabella!
OCTAVIUS CAESAR
    Let him alone, for I remember now
    How he's employ'd: he shall in time be ready.
    Go with me to my tent; where you shall see
    How hardly I was drawn into this war;
    How calm and gentle I proceeded still
    In all my writings: go with me, and see
    What I can show in this.

Exeunt

The Tragedie of Anthonie and Cleopatra — Act V

SCENE II.
Alexandria. A room in the monument.

Enter CLEOPATRA, CHARMIAN, and IRAS

CLEOPATRA
   My desolation does begin to make
   A better life. 'Tis paltry to be Caesar;
   Not being Fortune, he's but Fortune's knave,
   A minister of her will: and it is great
   To do that thing that ends all other deeds;
   Which shackles accidents and bolts up change;
   Which sleeps, and never palates more the dug,
   The beggar's nurse and Caesar's.

Enter, to the gates of the monument, PROCULEIUS, GALLUS and Soldiers

PROCULEIUS
   Caesar sends greeting to the Queen of Egypt;
   And bids thee study on what fair demands
   Thou mean'st to have him grant thee.
CLEOPATRA
   What's thy name?
PROCULEIUS
   My name is Proculeius.
CLEOPATRA
   Antony
   Did tell me of you, bade me trust you; but
   I do not greatly care to be deceived,
   That have no use for trusting. If your master
   Would have a queen his beggar, you must tell him,
   That majesty, to keep decorum, must
   No less beg than a kingdom: if he please
   To give me conquer'd Egypt for my son,

The Tragedie of Anthonie and Cleopatra — Act V

    He gives me so much of mine own, as I
    Will kneel to him with thanks.
PROCULEIUS
    Be of good cheer;
    You're fall'n into a princely hand, fear nothing:
    Make your full reference freely to my lord,
    Who is so full of grace, that it flows over
    On all that need: let me report to him
    Your sweet dependency; and you shall find
    A conqueror that will pray in aid for kindness,
    Where he for grace is kneel'd to.
CLEOPATRA
    Pray you, tell him
    I am his fortune's vassal, and I send him
    The greatness he has got. I hourly learn
    A doctrine of obedience; and would gladly
    Look him i' the face.
PROCULEIUS
    This I'll report, dear lady.
    Have comfort, for I know your plight is pitied
    Of him that caused it.
GALLUS
    You see how easily she may be surprised:

Here PROCULEIUS and two of the Guard ascend the monument by a ladder placed against a window, and, having descended, come behind CLEOPATRA. Some of the Guard unbar and open the gates

                    To PROCULEIUS and the Guard
    Guard her till Caesar come.

                                        Exit

IRAS
    Royal queen!

The Tragedie of Anthonie and Cleopatra — Act V

CHARMIAN
O Cleopatra! thou art taken, queen:
CLEOPATRA
Quick, quick, good hands.

Drawing a dagger

PROCULEIUS
Hold, worthy lady, hold:

Seizes and disarms her

Do not yourself such wrong, who are in this
Relieved, but not betray'd.
CLEOPATRA
What, of death too,
That rids our dogs of languish?
PROCULEIUS
Cleopatra,
Do not abuse my master's bounty by
The undoing of yourself: let the world see
His nobleness well acted, which your death
Will never let come forth.
CLEOPATRA
Where art thou, death?
Come hither, come! come, come, and take a queen
Worthy many babes and beggars!
PROCULEIUS
O, temperance, lady!
CLEOPATRA
Sir, I will eat no meat, I'll not drink, sir;
If idle talk will once be necessary,
I'll not sleep neither: this mortal house I'll ruin,
Do Caesar what he can. Know, sir, that I
Will not wait pinion'd at your master's court;
Nor once be chastised with the sober eye

The Tragedie of Anthonie and Cleopatra — Act V

    Of dull Octavia. Shall they hoist me up
    And show me to the shouting varletry
    Of censuring Rome? Rather a ditch in Egypt
    Be gentle grave unto me! rather on Nilus' mud
    Lay me stark naked, and let the water-flies
    Blow me into abhorring! rather make
    My country's high pyramides my gibbet,
    And hang me up in chains!
PROCULEIUS
    You do extend
    These thoughts of horror further than you shall
    Find cause in Caesar.

               Enter DOLABELLA

DOLABELLA
    Proculeius,
    What thou hast done thy master Caesar knows,
    And he hath sent for thee: for the queen,
    I'll take her to my guard.
PROCULEIUS
    So, Dolabella,
    It shall content me best: be gentle to her.
            To CLEOPATRA
    To Caesar I will speak what you shall please,
    If you'll employ me to him.

CLEOPATRA
    Say, I would die.

           Exeunt PROCULEIUS and Soldiers

DOLABELLA
    Most noble empress, you have heard of me?

The Tragedie of Anthonie and Cleopatra — Act V

CLEOPATRA
I cannot tell.
DOLABELLA
Assuredly you know me.
CLEOPATRA
No matter, sir, what I have heard or known.
You laugh when boys or women tell their dreams;
Is't not your trick?
DOLABELLA
I understand not, madam.
CLEOPATRA
I dream'd there was an Emperor Antony:
O, such another sleep, that I might see
But such another man!
DOLABELLA
If it might please ye,--
CLEOPATRA
His face was as the heavens; and therein stuck
A sun and moon, which kept their course,
and lighted
The little O, the earth.
DOLABELLA
Most sovereign creature,--
CLEOPATRA
His legs bestrid the ocean: his rear'd arm
Crested the world: his voice was propertied
As all the tuned spheres, and that to friends;
But when he meant to quail and shake the orb,
He was as rattling thunder. For his bounty,
There was no winter in't; an autumn 'twas
That grew the more by reaping: his delights
Were dolphin-like; they show'd his back above
The element they lived in: in his livery
Walk'd crowns and crownets; realms and islands were

The Tragedie of Anthonie and Cleopatra — Act V

    As plates dropp'd from his pocket.
DOLABELLA
    Cleopatra!
CLEOPATRA
    Think you there was, or might be, such a man
    As this I dream'd of?
DOLABELLA
    Gentle madam, no.
CLEOPATRA
    You lie, up to the hearing of the gods.
    But, if there be, or ever were, one such,
    It's past the size of dreaming: nature wants stuff
    To vie strange forms with fancy; yet, to imagine
    And Antony, were nature's piece 'gainst fancy,
    Condemning shadows quite.
DOLABELLA
    Hear me, good madam.
    Your loss is as yourself, great; and you bear it
    As answering to the weight: would I might never
    O'ertake pursued success, but I do feel,
    By the rebound of yours, a grief that smites
    My very heart at root.
CLEOPATRA
    I thank you, sir,
    Know you what Caesar means to do with me?
DOLABELLA
    I am loath to tell you what I would you knew.
CLEOPATRA
    Nay, pray you, sir,--
DOLABELLA
    Though he be honourable,--
CLEOPATRA
    He'll lead me, then, in triumph?

The Tragedie of Anthonie and Cleopatra — Act V

DOLABELLA
Madam, he will; I know't.

Flourish, and shout within, 'Make way there: Octavius Caesar!'

Enter OCTAVIUS CAESAR, GALLUS, PROCULEIUS, MECAENAS, SELEUCUS, and others of his Train

OCTAVIUS CAESAR
Which is the Queen of Egypt?
DOLABELLA
It is the emperor, madam.

CLEOPATRA kneels

OCTAVIUS CAESAR
Arise, you shall not kneel:
I pray you, rise; rise, Egypt.
CLEOPATRA
Sir, the gods
Will have it thus; my master and my lord
I must obey.
OCTAVIUS CAESAR
Take to you no hard thoughts:
The record of what injuries you did us,
Though written in our flesh, we shall remember
As things but done by chance.
CLEOPATRA
Sole sir o' the world,
I cannot project mine own cause so well
To make it clear; but do confess I have
Been laden with like frailties which before
Have often shamed our sex.
OCTAVIUS CAESAR
Cleopatra, know,

The Tragedie of Anthonie and Cleopatra — Act V

We will extenuate rather than enforce:
If you apply yourself to our intents,
Which towards you are most gentle, you shall find
A benefit in this change; but if you seek
To lay on me a cruelty, by taking
Antony's course, you shall bereave yourself
Of my good purposes, and put your children
To that destruction which I'll guard them from,
If thereon you rely. I'll take my leave.

CLEOPATRA

And may, through all the world: 'tis yours; and we,
Your scutcheons and your signs of conquest, shall
Hang in what place you please. Here, my good lord.

OCTAVIUS CAESAR

You shall advise me in all for Cleopatra.

CLEOPATRA

This is the brief of money, plate, and jewels,
I am possess'd of: 'tis exactly valued;
Not petty things admitted. Where's Seleucus?

SELEUCUS

Here, madam.

CLEOPATRA

This is my treasurer: let him speak, my lord,
Upon his peril, that I have reserved
To myself nothing. Speak the truth, Seleucus.

SELEUCUS

Madam,
I had rather seal my lips, than, to my peril,
Speak that which is not.

CLEOPATRA

What have I kept back?

SELEUCUS

Enough to purchase what you have made known.

The Tragedie of Anthonie and Cleopatra — Act V

OCTAVIUS CAESAR
  Nay, blush not, Cleopatra; I approve
  Your wisdom in the deed.

CLEOPATRA
  See, Caesar! O, behold,
  How pomp is follow'd! mine will now be yours;
  And, should we shift estates, yours would be mine.
  The ingratitude of this Seleucus does
  Even make me wild: O slave, of no more trust
  Than love that's hired! What, goest thou back? thou shalt
  Go back, I warrant thee; but I'll catch thine eyes,
  Though they had wings: slave, soulless villain, dog!
  O rarely base!

OCTAVIUS CAESAR
  Good queen, let us entreat you.

CLEOPATRA
  O Caesar, what a wounding shame is this,
  That thou, vouchsafing here to visit me,
  Doing the honour of thy lordliness
  To one so meek, that mine own servant should
  Parcel the sum of my disgraces by
  Addition of his envy! Say, good Caesar,
  That I some lady trifles have reserved,
  Immoment toys, things of such dignity
  As we greet modern friends withal; and say,
  Some nobler token I have kept apart
  For Livia and Octavia, to induce
  Their mediation; must I be unfolded
  With one that I have bred? The gods! it smites me
  Beneath the fall I have.
      To SELEUCUS
  Prithee, go hence;
  Or I shall show the cinders of my spirits
  Through the ashes of my chance: wert thou a man,

The Tragedie of Anthonie and Cleopatra — Act V

    Thou wouldst have mercy on me.
OCTAVIUS CAESAR
    Forbear, Seleucus.

Exit SELEUCUS

CLEOPATRA
    Be it known, that we, the greatest, are misthought
    For things that others do; and, when we fall,
    We answer others' merits in our name,
    Are therefore to be pitied.
OCTAVIUS CAESAR
    Cleopatra,
    Not what you have reserved, nor what acknowledged,
    Put we i' the roll of conquest: still be't yours,
    Bestow it at your pleasure; and believe,
    Caesar's no merchant, to make prize with you
    Of things that merchants sold. Therefore be cheer'd;
    Make not your thoughts your prisons: no, dear queen;
    For we intend so to dispose you as
    Yourself shall give us counsel. Feed, and sleep:
    Our care and pity is so much upon you,
    That we remain your friend; and so, adieu.
CLEOPATRA
    My master, and my lord!
OCTAVIUS CAESAR
    Not so. Adieu.

Flourish. Exeunt OCTAVIUS CAESAR and his train

CLEOPATRA
    He words me, girls, he words me, that I should not
    Be noble to myself: but, hark thee, Charmian.

Whispers CHARMIAN

The Tragedie of Anthonie and Cleopatra — Act V

IRAS
   Finish, good lady; the bright day is done,
   And we are for the dark.
CLEOPATRA
   Hie thee again:
   I have spoke already, and it is provided;
   Go put it to the haste.
CHARMIAN
   Madam, I will.

Re-enter DOLABELLA

DOLABELLA
   Where is the queen?
CHARMIAN
   Behold, sir.

Exit

CLEOPATRA
   Dolabella!
DOLABELLA
   Madam, as thereto sworn by your command,
   Which my love makes religion to obey,
   I tell you this: Caesar through Syria
   Intends his journey; and within three days
   You with your children will he send before:
   Make your best use of this: I have perform'd
   Your pleasure and my promise.
CLEOPATRA
   Dolabella,
   I shall remain your debtor.
DOLABELLA
   I your servant,
   Adieu, good queen; I must attend on Caesar.

CLEOPATRA
 Farewell, and thanks.

 Exit DOLABELLA

 Now, Iras, what think'st thou?
 Thou, an Egyptian puppet, shalt be shown
 In Rome, as well as I mechanic slaves
 With greasy aprons, rules, and hammers, shall
 Uplift us to the view; in their thick breaths,
 Rank of gross diet, shall be enclouded,
 And forced to drink their vapour.
IRAS
 The gods forbid!
CLEOPATRA
 Nay, 'tis most certain, Iras: saucy lictors
 Will catch at us, like strumpets; and scald rhymers
 Ballad us out o' tune: the quick comedians
 Extemporally will stage us, and present
 Our Alexandrian revels; Antony
 Shall be brought drunken forth, and I shall see
 Some squeaking Cleopatra boy my greatness
 I' the posture of a whore.
IRAS
 O the good gods!
CLEOPATRA
 Nay, that's certain.
IRAS
 I'll never see 't; for, I am sure, my nails
 Are stronger than mine eyes.
CLEOPATRA
 Why, that's the way
 To fool their preparation, and to conquer
 Their most absurd intents.

 Re-enter CHARMIAN

The Tragedie of Anthonie and Cleopatra — Act V

Now, Charmian!
Show me, my women, like a queen: go fetch
My best attires: I am again for Cydnus,
To meet Mark Antony: sirrah Iras, go.
Now, noble Charmian, we'll dispatch indeed;
And, when thou hast done this chare, I'll give thee leave
To play till doomsday. Bring our crown and all.
Wherefore's this noise?

Exit IRAS. A noise within

Enter a Guardsman

Guard
　Here is a rural fellow
　That will not be denied your highness presence:
　He brings you figs.
CLEOPATRA
　Let him come in.

Exit Guardsman

What poor an instrument
May do a noble deed! he brings me liberty.
My resolution's placed, and I have nothing
Of woman in me: now from head to foot
I am marble-constant; now the fleeting moon
No planet is of mine.

Re-enter Guardsman, with Clown bringing in a basket

Guard
　This is the man.

CLEOPATRA
　Avoid, and leave him.

Exit Guardsman

Hast thou the pretty worm of Nilus there,
That kills and pains not?

Clown

Truly, I have him: but I would not be the party
that should desire you to touch him, for his biting
is immortal; those that do die of it do seldom or
never recover.

CLEOPATRA

Rememberest thou any that have died on't?

Clown

Very many, men and women too. I heard of one of
them no longer than yesterday: a very honest woman,
but something given to lie; as a woman should not
do, but in the way of honesty: how she died of the
biting of it, what pain she felt: truly, she makes
a very good report o' the worm; but he that will
believe all that they say, shall never be saved by
half that they do: but this is most fallible, the
worm's an odd worm.

CLEOPATRA

Get thee hence; farewell.

Clown

I wish you all joy of the worm.

Setting down his basket

CLEOPATRA

Farewell.

Clown

You must think this, look you, that the worm will
do his kind.

CLEOPATRA

Ay, ay; farewell.

Clown

Look you, the worm is not to be trusted but in the

The Tragedie of Anthonie and Cleopatra — Act V

keeping of wise people; for, indeed, there is no goodness in worm.

CLEOPATRA

Take thou no care; it shall be heeded.

Clown

Very good. Give it nothing, I pray you, for it is not worth the feeding.

CLEOPATRA

Will it eat me?

Clown

You must not think I am so simple but I know the devil himself will not eat a woman: I know that a woman is a dish for the gods, if the devil dress her not. But, truly, these same whoreson devils do the gods great harm in their women; for in every ten that they make, the devils mar five.

CLEOPATRA

Well, get thee gone; farewell.

Clown

Yes, forsooth: I wish you joy o' the worm.

Exit

Re-enter IRAS with a robe, crown, & c

CLEOPATRA

Give me my robe, put on my crown; I have
Immortal longings in me: now no more
The juice of Egypt's grape shall moist this lip:
Yare, yare, good Iras; quick. Methinks I hear
Antony call; I see him rouse himself
To praise my noble act; I hear him mock
The luck of Caesar, which the gods give men
To excuse their after wrath: husband, I come:

The Tragedie of Anthonie and Cleopatra — Act V

Now to that name my courage prove my title!
I am fire and air; my other elements
I give to baser life. So; have you done?
Come then, and take the last warmth of my lips.
Farewell, kind Charmian; Iras, long farewell.

Kisses them. IRAS falls and dies

Have I the aspic in my lips? Dost fall?
If thou and nature can so gently part,
The stroke of death is as a lover's pinch,
Which hurts, and is desired. Dost thou lie still?
If thus thou vanishest, thou tell'st the world
It is not worth leave-taking.

CHARMIAN

Dissolve, thick cloud, and rain; that I may say,
The gods themselves do weep!

CLEOPATRA

This proves me base:
If she first meet the curled Antony,
He'll make demand of her, and spend that kiss
Which is my heaven to have. Come, thou mortal wretch,

To an asp, which she applies to her breast

With thy sharp teeth this knot intrinsicate
Of life at once untie: poor venomous fool
Be angry, and dispatch. O, couldst thou speak,
That I might hear thee call great Caesar ass
Unpolicied!

CHARMIAN

O eastern star!

CLEOPATRA

Peace, peace!
Dost thou not see my baby at my breast,
That sucks the nurse asleep?

The Tragedie of Anthonie and Cleopatra — Act V

CHARMIAN
O, break! O, break!
CLEOPATRA
As sweet as balm, as soft as air, as gentle,--
O Antony!--Nay, I will take thee too.

Applying another asp to her arm

What should I stay--

Dies

CHARMIAN
In this vile world? So, fare thee well.
Now boast thee, death, in thy possession lies
A lass unparallel'd. Downy windows, close;
And golden Phoebus never be beheld
Of eyes again so royal! Your crown's awry;
I'll mend it, and then play.

Enter the Guard, rushing in

First Guard
Where is the queen?
CHARMIAN
Speak softly, wake her not.
First Guard
Caesar hath sent--
CHARMIAN
Too slow a messenger.

Applies an asp

O, come apace, dispatch! I partly feel thee.
First Guard
Approach, ho! All's not well: Caesar's beguiled.
Second Guard
There's Dolabella sent from Caesar; call him.

First Guard
   What work is here! Charmian, is this well done?
CHARMIAN
   It is well done, and fitting for a princess
   Descended of so many royal kings.
   Ah, soldier!

Dies

Re-enter DOLABELLA

DOLABELLA
   How goes it here?
Second Guard
   All dead.
DOLABELLA
   Caesar, thy thoughts
   Touch their effects in this: thyself art coming
   To see perform'd the dreaded act which thou
   So sought'st to hinder.

Within: 'A way there, a way for Caesar!'

Re-enter OCTAVIUS CAESAR and all his train marching

DOLABELLA
   O sir, you are too sure an augurer;
   That you did fear is done.
OCTAVIUS CAESAR
   Bravest at the last,
   She levell'd at our purposes, and, being royal,
   Took her own way. The manner of their deaths?
   I do not see them bleed.
DOLABELLA
   Who was last with them?
First Guard
   A simple countryman, that brought her figs:

The Tragedie of Anthonie and Cleopatra — Act V

This was his basket.
OCTAVIUS CAESAR
  Poison'd, then.
First Guard
  O Caesar,
  This Charmian lived but now; she stood and spake:
  I found her trimming up the diadem
  On her dead mistress; tremblingly she stood
  And on the sudden dropp'd.
OCTAVIUS CAESAR
  O noble weakness!
  If they had swallow'd poison, 'twould appear
  By external swelling: but she looks like sleep,
  As she would catch another Antony
  In her strong toil of grace.
DOLABELLA
  Here, on her breast,
  There is a vent of blood and something blown:
  The like is on her arm.
First Guard
  This is an aspic's trail: and these fig-leaves
  Have slime upon them, such as the aspic leaves
  Upon the caves of Nile.
OCTAVIUS CAESAR
  Most probable
  That so she died; for her physician tells me
  She hath pursued conclusions infinite
  Of easy ways to die. Take up her bed;
  And bear her women from the monument:
  She shall be buried by her Antony:
  No grave upon the earth shall clip in it
  A pair so famous. High events as these
  Strike those that make them; and their story is
  No less in pity than his glory which

The Tragedie of Anthonie and Cleopatra — Act V

Brought them to be lamented. Our army shall
In solemn show attend this funeral;
And then to Rome. Come, Dolabella, see
High order in this great solemnity.

Exeunt

Hedingham Castle
The Birthplace of Edward de Vere

The manor of Hedingham was awarded to Aubrey de Vere I by William the Conqueror sometime before 1086. The castle was constructed by the de Veres in the late 11th and early 12th centuries, and the Keep (shown) in the 1130s and 1140s. It is the only part of the castle that has survived. The castle was held by the de Vere family until 1625.

Today, the castle is the residence of the Lindsay family, direct descendants of the de Veres, but it is also used as a striking venue for educational tours and other public and private events. Short of a personal visit, it's possible to take the most captivating '3D Virtual Tour' at the Hedingham Castle website:
> https://www.hedinghamcastle.co.uk/visit
> (Scroll down to find the tour.)

Biography

A Short Life of Edward de Vere, 17th Earl of Oxford

by Dr. Kevin Gilvary, President
The de Vere Society

He was born on 12 April 1550 at Castle Hedingham, his family's ancestral home. His father, John de Vere, 16th Earl, was Lord Great Chamberlain and attended the coronations of both Mary and Elizabeth Tudor. His mother was Margaret Golding. Edward was 11 when, in 1561, Queen Elizabeth visited Hedingham for four days of masques, feasting and entertainments. When his father died in 1562, young Oxford left to become, like Bertram in *All's Well that Ends Well*, a ward of the Crown under the guardianship of William Cecil, the Queen's private secretary (later Lord Burghley, Lord Treasurer). His mother married Charles Tyrrell and seems to have passed out of the boy's life. His sister Mary went to live with her stepfather and the siblings were not reunited for some years.

According to a curriculum in Cecil's own hand, Edward de Vere's daily studies included dancing, French, Latin, writing and drawing, cosmography, penmanship, riding, shooting, exercise and prayer. Edward de Vere showed a prodigious talent for scholarship from his early years, and we may ascribe his lifelong love of learning to the influence of two of his early tutors. The first was Sir Thomas Smith who was, perhaps, England's most respected Greek scholar and the former Cambridge tutor of Sir William Cecil. It was, no doubt, through Cecil's influence that Edward de Vere spent some time living in the household of Smith in his early years, during which time he spent about five months at Smith's alma mater, Queens' College, Cambridge. Smith was a scholar of widely varied interests – this was reflected in his 400-volume library, some of which is still extant at Cambridge. De Vere's other tutor was Laurence Nowell, who was not only an accomplished cartographer but was also England's premier scholar of Anglo-Saxon literature – it was Nowell who possessed the only known copy of *Beowulf*.

Another important influence on Edward de Vere's early studies was his maternal uncle Arthur Golding, an officer in the Court of Wards under Cecil, who is credited with the translation of Ovid's *Metamorphoses*, published in 1567, a book widely recognised as having a major influence on 'Shakespeare'.

Following on from his matriculation at Cambridge in November 1558, Edward was awarded an honorary MA by Cambridge during a Royal progress in August 1564, and another degree by Oxford University during a Royal progress in 1566. Edward de Vere then attended Gray's Inn to study law. One notable feature of the Elizabethan Inns of Court was a tradition of mounting dramatic productions and of hosting the various touring companies of players.

In 1570 he served in a military campaign in Scotland under the Earl of Sussex. By 1571, he was reported as a leading luminary of the Court and, for a time, a favourite of Queen Elizabeth. In December 1571 he married Anne Cecil, aged 15, daughter of his guardian. This was a dynastic marriage where all the advantage accrued to Cecil who, ennobled as Baron Burghley, had reduced the social gap between himself and the young Earl.

While Oxford was away on a Grand Tour of Europe, he heard that his daughter Elizabeth Vere had been born in July 1575. On his return in early 1576, he appeared to have been convinced that Elizabeth was not his child; consequently he became estranged from Anne for five years, and exiled himself from Court, taking up residence in the Savoy and concerning himself with literary and musical patronage.

Already, in 1573, *Cardanus Comfort* (the Consolations of Boethius) had been translated from Latin by Thomas Bedingfield and dedicated to Oxford; and published with a preface written by him. In 1576 an anthology, *A Paradise of Daintie Devices*, including several poems by Oxford, was published. These are juvenile works but already show affinities, in both style and thought, with those of the mature Shakespeare.

Oxford's Grand Tour had taken in Paris, Strasbourg, Venice, Genoa, Florence, Palermo and, on his way back through France, Rousillon – the setting for *Love's Labour's Lost*. Oxford spent the best part of a year travelling in Italy in 1576, and becoming involved with moneylenders. He came back to England fluent in Italian and well acquainted with the northern Italian cities, to be satirised by Gabriel Harvey as 'The Italian Earl'. On his way back his ship was attacked by pirates in the English Channel (cf. *Hamlet*). Fourteen of 'Shakespeare's' plays have Italian settings, in which he put his detailed knowledge of the country, beyond pure book knowledge, to good use.

1573 saw the birth of Henry Wriothesley, Earl of Southampton. Although history has not bequeathed to us any evidence of a direct relationship between the two men, in the relatively small world of the royal Court, they must have been acquainted with each other. The poems *Venus and Adonis* (1593) and *The Rape of Lucrece* (1594) were dedicated to Southampton. These were the first works to be published under the name 'Shakespeare' and for the next five years the records show the byline 'Shakespeare' to have been associated exclusively with these two poems. Plays under the name 'Shakespeare' did not appear in print until 1598, the year that Lord Burghley died.

In May 1577 Oxford invested in Frobisher's voyage in the ship *Edward Bonaventure*. Despite its name, the ship's voyage across the Atlantic in search of the North-West Passage lost money; consequently he was forced to sell three estates (cf. Hamlet's words 'I am but mad north-north-west' II.1.). In 1578 he invested in Frobisher's second expedition, which also lost money, forcing further sales of estates.

He was mentioned by Gabriel Harvey in an address to Queen Elizabeth in July 1578, as a prolific private poet and one 'whose countenance shakes spears'. In the same year John Lyly, Oxford's secretary, published *Euphues.The Anatomy of Wit*, followed in 1579 by *Euphues and his England*, dedicated to Oxford. These two books launched the fashion for 'Euphuism', a style characterized by high-flown language, satirized in *Love's Labour's Lost*.

In March 1581 Oxford's mistress, Anne Vavasour, who was one of Queen Elizabeth's Ladies of the Bedchamber, gave birth to a son. The lovers and their son were sent to the Tower by an infuriated Queen but swiftly released (cf. *Measure for Measure*). After his release, Oxford was wounded in a street-fight provoked by Thomas Knyvet, a kinsman of Anne Vavasour; affrays continued in the streets of London between the rival gangs of supporters for over a year (cf.*Romeo and Juliet*).

In December 1581 he resumed living with his long-suffering and devoted wife, and accepted Elizabeth

Vere as his child. Tragically, their only son died one day after his birth. Three more daughters followed, of whom Susan and Bridget survived.

In 1584, Robert Greene's *Gwydonius; the Card of Fancy* was dedicated to him, identifying him as a 'pre-eminent writer'. In 1586, when he was 36, he served on the tribunal which condemned Mary, Queen of Scots to execution.

In the same year, the Queen awarded Oxford an unconditional pension of £1,000 a year for life (about £500,000 at today's value). The motive for this uncharacteristic generosity on the part of the Queen remains a mystery – no accounting was required of Oxford. Her successor, King James I, continued to pay the pension. In reply to Sir Robert Cecil's request that Lord Sheffield's pension be increased, the King refused, saying, 'Great Oxford got no more . . .', leaving us to wonder why Great Oxford? His greatness does not seem to have resided in war or any of the known offices of State. Perhaps a clue can be found in a letter to Burghley, written in 1594, in which Edward de Vere seeks his favour in a matter involving what he describes as 'in mine office' and that this office is beholden to the Queen.

In 1589, George Puttenham published *The Arte of English Poesie* and this contains the most telling recognition of Edward de Vere's literary standing amongst his contemporaries: 'And in her Majesties time that now is are sprong up an other crew of Courtly makers Noble men and Gentlemen of her Majesties owne servantes, who have written excellently well as it would appear if their doings could be found out and made publicke with the rest, of which number is first that noble Gentleman Edward Earle of Oxford.'

In 1588 his wife Anne, daughter of Lord Burghley, died and in extant letters written at this time, it is reported that Burghley is so incapacitated by grief over the death of his favourite daughter that he is incapable of conducting any Privy Council business.

Three years later, in 1591, Oxford married another of the Queen's Maids of Honour, Elizabeth Trentham, with whom he finally became the father of a male heir; Henry de Vere, 18th Earl of Oxford. Although there is evidence of his continued involvement in Court affairs, from the date of this marriage Edward de Vere's life at his new home at King's Place in Hackney is perhaps the most obscure of his entire life.

In 1594, his ship the *Edward Bonaventure* was wrecked in Bermuda (cf. *The Tempest*). In January 1595, Elizabeth Vere married William Stanley, 6th Earl of Derby, another literary earl who maintained his own company of players – many scholars believe that *A Midsummer Night's Dream* was written for these festivities which were attended by the whole royal Court.

On September 7 1598, Francis Meres' *Palladis Tamia* was registered for publication, naming Oxford as the 'best for comedy'. This is a vital document in Shakespearean history because it includes the first mention of 'Shakespeare' as a playwright, attributing twelve plays to him; until then Shakespeare's reputation had rested on the two narrative poems only.

Oxford suffered all his life from financial difficulties, much of which can be traced to the fact that Queen Elizabeth handed out the bulk of his estate to her favourite courtier the Earl of Leicester during Oxford's minority as a royal ward (estates which Oxford found almost impossible to reclaim), and the ruinous debt she placed upon him over his marriage to Anne Cecil. It is, however, notable that his new brother-in-law, the wealthy Staffordshire landowner and Knight of the Shire Francis Trentham, took over the management of Edward de

Vere's near-bankrupt estate from 1591 and gradually nursed it back to health so that, when Oxford died, all of his massive debts had been cleared.

On the Queen's death in 1603 Oxford wrote eloquently to Sir Robert Cecil, son and heir of Lord Burghley, of his 'great grief'. He wrote, 'In this common shipwreck, mine is above all the rest, who least regarded, though often comforted, she hath left to try my fortune among the alterations of time and chance'.

Oxford died in Hackney in 1604, cause unknown. Parish records state that he was buried in Hackney Church on July 6, but a family history by his first cousin Percival Golding, states 'Edward de Veer … a man in mind and body absolutely accomplished with honorable endowments … lieth buried at Westminster'. No record of such a burial can now be traced in Westminster Abbey, where there is a Vere family tomb.

The Aftermath of Oxford's life and death

During the winter season 1604-05, six of Shakespeare's plays were presented at Court by command of King James I. This has an air of commemoration. In 1609 the *Sonnets* were published in a pirated edition. The famous dedication describes the author as 'our ever-living', a phrase invariably used only of the dead.

In 1622 Henry Peacham published, in *The Compleat Gentelman*, a list of poets who made Elizabeth's reign a 'golden age'. Unaccountably, he omitted Shakespeare but placed the Earl of Oxford in first place in his list – perhaps he knew them to be the same person. This is unlike Meres who included them both – maybe one reason was because he didn't know Oxford and Shakespeare were the same person.

We do not know who instigated publication of the First Folio Edition of the Shakespeare plays in 1623, but there is no mention of any executor or relative of Shakspere of Stratford in connection with it. However, of the two brothers who financed it and to whom it was dedicated, one – Philip Earl of Montgomery – was the husband of Oxford's daughter Susan, while the other – William Earl of Pembroke – had once been a suitor for her sister Bridget. Pembroke was Lord Chamberlain, the supreme authority in the world of theatre, and thus in a position to decide which plays were to be published and which suppressed. We also know that Ben Jonson, who wrote much of the introductory material, was an intimate associate of the de Vere family after Oxford's death. The First Folio was therefore very much a family affair, but the family was not the one in Stratford-on-Avon.

Coat of Arms of Edward de Vere, 17th Earl of Oxford

Vero Nihil Verius
Nothing is Truer than [de] Vere [Truth]

This is the coat of arms that was fashioned for [by] Edward himself in 1574 and published in the medical book of the de Vere family physician, George Baker, entitled *Oleum Magistrale*. This dedication of his book to Edward de Vere on the part of Dr. Baker is thought to be in recognition of Edward's expertise in the medical sciences as well as in the traditions of heraldry that are so much in evidence throughout his plays and poetry.

An AfterVerse

For those with yet an interest
In strenuous debate
We've compiled a list of books and films
Your appetite to sate.
From this study clear your mind
Of doubt and all misgiving-
Who from us has long since gone
And who is ever-living.

Selected References & Bibliography
About the Author
Edward de Vere, 17th Earl of Oxford

Books

♦ Anderson, M. (2005). *Shakespeare by Another Name: The Life of Edward de Vere, Earl of Oxford, The Man who was Shakespeare.* New York: Gotham Books.
--A physicist by training with research interest in how evidence supports or negates a theory, Mark Anderson spent ten years investigating Edward de Vere as the author of Shake-speare's works.

♦Farina, William. (2006). *De Vere as Shakespeare: An Oxfordian Reading of the Canon.*
Jefferson, NC. McFarland & Company.

--Each of the plays and poems is individually assessed and explored in its own chapter, using the innumerable connections between the text itself and the life of its author, Edward de Vere.

♦ Looney, J. Thomas (2018). *Shakespeare Identified.* Cary, N.C. Veritas Publicaations.
--First published in 1920 this book began the modern Oxfordian movement. From reading it, Sigmund Freud became convinced and John Galsworthy called it "the best detective story I ever read."

♦ Ogburn, C. (1992). *The Mysterious William Shakespeare.* McLean (Va.): EPM.
--An in depth exploration and must read foundational book on the authorship question.

♦Sobran, Joseph. (1997). *Alias Shakespeare: Solving the Greatest Literary Mystery of All Time.* New York; The Free Press, A Division of Simon & Schuster.
--A concise exploration of the puzzling questions surrounding the authorship controversy with the evidence decisively supporting the case for Edward de Vere, the 17th Earl of Oxford, as the rightful author of the Shakespeare plays and poems.

♦Whittemore, Hank. (2016), *100 Reasons Shake-speare Was the Earl of Oxford.* Somerville MA. Forever Press.
►Also with further discussion and public comment at: *Hank Whittemore's Shakespeare Blog.*
https://hankwhittemore.com/
--In both the book and online blog cited above, Whittemore presents a concise introduction to the

authorship question that examines 100 different aspects, from biographical and historical records, that point to Edward de Vere as the true writer of the Shake-speare plays and poems.

Websites & Videos

▶ De Vere Society. (2019). The de Vere Society – Dedicated to the proposition that the works of Shakespeare were written by Edward de Vere, 17th Earl of Oxford. [online] Deveresociety.co.uk. Available at: https://deveresociety.co.uk
--*A very complete resource with substantial biographical and authorship information and links.*

▶ The Oxford Fellowship (2019). Shakespeare Oxford Fellowship | Research and Discussion of the Shakespeare Authorship Question. [online] Shakespeare Oxford Fellowship. Available at: https://shakespeareoxfordfellowship.org/
--*A seminal online resource especially focusing on the authorship question.*

▶ Waugh, A. (2019). Alexander Waugh. [online] YouTube. Available at: https://www.youtube.com/channel/UCHN7SCKlsa9lPYJmqqQ2uIg/featured/
OR simply search: 'Alexander Waugh'
--*Alexander Waugh is a leading authorship scholar who has produced many fascinating video presentations on the authorship question. This link is to his YouTube Channel.*

▶ Columbia Pictures & Centropolis Entertainment. (2011). *Anonymous.* Produced and directed by Roland Emmerich. [DVD]
--This mainstream film is both entertaining and enlightening. It presents a superb dramatization of the character of Edward de Vere, setting out in detail the historical and personal context which made his anonymous authorship necessary.

▶Centropolis Entertainment and First Folio Pictures. *Last Will and Testament.* (2012). [DVD]
--A thoughtful and ground-breaking video documentary introduction to the Shakespeare authorship question.

Acknowledgment

Our sincere thanks to
The de Vere Society
and
The Shakespeare Oxford Fellowship
for their inspiration, help and support
in creating this series.

Attributions

--*Character list from Wikipedia under
the Creative Commons License 3.0*
--*Play text from the Moby(tm) editions
in the public domain*

Photos

Coat of Arms of Edward de Vere
Source: Wikimedia.org
Author: George Baker / Public domain

The Keep at Castle Hedingham
Source: geograph.org.uk
Author: David Phillips / CC BY-SA 2.0

Cover inset: *Cleopatra with the Snake.* 1897
by Theodor Matthei, Oil on canvas, Public domain

This work has been edited and produced by
Verus Publishing
www.verusbooks.com

www.ingramcontent.com/pod-product-compliance
Lightning Source LLC
Chambersburg PA
CBHW031629160426
43196CB00006B/337